P O L A R I S

Children on Rhu Spit, waving goodbye.

POLARIS

THE HISTORY OF THE UK'S SUBMARINE FORCE

KEITH HALL

The History Press

All royalties raised from the sale of this book are being donated to the Friends of the Submarine Museum

First published 2018
Reprinted 2020

The History Press
97 St George's Place, Cheltenham,
Gloucestershire, GL50 3QB
www.thehistorypress.co.uk

British Library Cataloguing in Publication Data.
A catalogue record for this book is available from the British Library.

ISBN 978 0 7524 5177 0

Typesetting and origination by The History Press
Printed in Great Britain by TJ International Ltd, Padstow, Cornwall.

CONTENTS

FOREWORD

The United Kingdom's independent strategic nuclear deterrent is a weapon of peace, not war. Throughout the period known as the Cold War, the Polaris weapon system in various forms of upgraded capability was on continuous deployment, ready at all times to retaliate to a pre-emptive nuclear attack on the United Kingdom or members of the NATO alliance. The unimaginable outcome of an attack of this kind, the inevitability of mutually assured destruction (MAD), deterred the use of nuclear release during its in-service life and after with the introduction of the Trident weapon system.

I am honoured to pen the foreword to this most informative and personal salute to the Polaris project, which stands alone as an example of managerial, logistical and leadership competency, both in its planning and execution. A project of this magnitude and complexity has not been equalled since. Not only did the team procure a completely new major weapon system under that very special relationship with the United States but they designed and built the submarines to carry them. To house all this, they constructed the two sizeable bases to support these submarines and their weapons, and provided the especially trained personnel to man them. The submarines came on stream in June 1968 and carried the national deterrent until May 1996, when the responsibility passed to the Trident weapon system. The four Polaris submarines of the 10th Submarine Squadron carried out a total of 229 operational patrols, their unbroken service ensuring that the UK's nuclear deterrent was available and ready to launch at all times.

My own submarine service spanned the Cold War years from 1969 to 1994, during which time I spent eighteen years in support of the Polaris deterrent both at sea and ashore. First I became an integral part of the strategic weapon system as the navigating officer of HMS *Resolution*, then gained further experience as an executive officer, before holding a key operational planning role at Polaris headquarters in Northwood. I had successful command of HMS *Repulse*, launching a batch of y missiles at the US demonstration and shakedown facility at Cape Canaveral, then a second command, of HMS *Revenge*, before an MoD appointment to the Nuclear Policy Directorate. A committed believer in the independent strategic nuclear deterrent, I would not have missed a day in its service.

The author also spent the majority of his submarine service in support of the Polaris weapon system, part of that unique team providing continuous at sea deterrence. It was during the long periods at sea on patrol that hobbies were indulged. Some members of the ships' companies chose model making, others took up art projects, some studied for Open University degrees and Keith Hall developed his interest in submarine history, in time publishing a series of books and articles about submarines and their supporting bases. This book is a comprehensive record of the incredible Polaris project from inception to replacement. Keith is a firm believer that the rapid development of the UK Polaris fleet and its timely operational deployment was a truly outstanding political and management achievement only made possible by the determination and leadership of Admiral Sir 'Rufus' Mackenzie KCB, DSO, DSC a former flag officer submarines appointed Chief Polaris Executive, responsible to the Controller of the Navy, an equally talented Vice Admiral Sir Michael Le Fanu GCB DSC. They were a formidable couple.

The early chapters of this book chart the history of the United Kingdom's international relationships, periods of conflict, development of war fighting capability and the complexities of political discord that resulted in the Iron Curtain dividing Europe. From this grew the need to establish a defence mechanism through deterrence. The creation of the independent strategic nuclear deterrent is catalogued in detail, including details of the political and technical exchanges between the UK, USA and France before the decision was made bilaterally to proceed with Polaris. Thereafter, we are shown the 'Who's Who' of the 10th Submarine Squadron when it was reformed in 1967 and the lists of commanding officers of the four

Resolution Class submarines. The reader is then treated to a guided tour of a Polaris submarine and an insight into the way our lives were conducted in support of this unique part of the UK's military capability. For the curious, this is perhaps the most interesting section as it answers the questions so frequently asked: What does it feel like to be underwater? Do you ever suffer from claustrophobia? What happens if you go sick? What is the food like? What would you feel if you had to fire these missiles for real? With all that time spent in the system there will be so many anecdotes to record and tell. Perhaps this will appear in time as an amusing sequel to a very serious but proud story.

Bob Seaward OBE
A Bomber Man

INTRODUCTION

The world immediately after the Second World War was a very different place to the one we know today, even with all its uncertainties and insecurities. Although Russia, America and Britain had been allies during the last four years of the war, it would be fair to say it was a far from harmonious relationship and disagreements that had existed throughout the war continued and even intensified after the defeat of Germany. Age old cultural and political differences between East and West came to the fore, only this time as a result of contradictory interests, misinterpretations and especially the introduction of nuclear weapons. The troubles between the super-powers reached new heights and resulted in a self-perpetuating, spiralling competition to better one another. Looking back, even over this relatively short period of time, it is hard to imagine the feelings of apprehension and foreboding that were felt throughout Europe after the Second World War. Countries were shattered and their people's hopes of a peace, a new just world, were not realised, or at best, would take some time to materialise. In Britain, a victor of the war, cities lay devastated, rationing was still in force and was to remain so until 1953; the country was all but bankrupt. Was this the country that so many people had died defending? It was no fit place for heroes.

After the war, most of Europe was occupied by the three victorious countries. The Russians created an Eastern Bloc of countries, annexing some as Soviet socialist republics, in others they installed puppet governments, and these satellite states would later form the Warsaw Pact. In other parts of the world, Latin America and Southeast Asia, for example, Russia encouraged

Communist revolutionary movements. Needless to say, America and many of its allies opposed this and, in some cases, attempted to obstruct or even topple these puppet regimes. America and various Western European countries began a policy of containment, which became known as the Truman Doctrine, in an attempt at a European Recovery Programme (ERP). This was a plan to aid Western Europe in which America gave $13 billion (approximately $130 billion in today's money) in economic support to help rebuild Western European economies after the end of the war. Several alliances were forged to combat the Russian threat, most noticeably the formation of the North Atlantic Treaty Organisation (NATO) on 4 April 1947.

In the years after the war the Russians were making threatening radio broadcasts into Finland, while revolts that broke out against the communist governments in East Germany in 1953 and in Poland in 1956 were ruthlessly put down. Also in 1956, Hungary was invaded after trying to break free from Russian control. American nuclear-armed Thor missiles were stationed in Eastern England. All this added to the general atmosphere of distrust, cynicism and concern that prevailed throughout much of the world and was further fuelled by politicians' responses to events that they did not properly understand. Public fears reached new heights during the Cuban missile crisis in October 1962, a thirteen-day confrontation between America and the Soviet Union when Russian ballistic missiles were deployed in Cuba. I remember reading about an RAF officer who was stationed at a Thor missile battery at this time, when these missiles were at full alert ready to launch. He was stood down for a few hours and took the opportunity to go home and see his family, who lived nearby. When he got there he was surprised to see his young children playing with their Christmas presents on the front lawn. He asked his wife why she had given the children presents early. She told him she was so worried about the current world situation that she was convinced none of them would be alive at Christmas. She certainly wasn't alone in this view.

Although the two prime contenders never fought one another directly, there were several proxy wars and unimaginably vast amounts of money were spent on espionage, weapon developments, propaganda and competitive technological development, the most obvious of which was the space race. Initially the responsibility for the Cold War was placed on the Russians; Stalin had broken promises he made at Yalta by imposing

Russian-dominated regimes on reluctant Eastern European states. Also, his paranoia and ego did little to quell Western fears and this was further increased by his stated aim to spread communism throughout the world. This left America and her allies with little option but to respond.

During the 1960s an alternative view was proposed. It was claimed that America had made efforts to isolate and confront Russia well before the end of the Second World War. The main motivation was the promotion of capitalism and to this end they pursued a policy that guaranteed an open door to foreign markets for American business and agriculture across the world. It was reasoned that a growing domestic economy would lead to a bolstering of American influence and power internationally. It has also been stated that the Russian occupation of Eastern Europe might have had a defensive rationale, enabling the Russians to avoid 'encirclement' by America and its allies; it would also provide a buffer zone against invasion. It was argued that Russia was devastated, both physically and financially, at the end of the Second World War; it was highly unlikely she could pose a credible threat to America, particularly as at this time, America was the only country with the atomic bomb. However, in view of Russia's actions after the war it is particularly difficult to support these arguments. Controlling repressive governments need an enemy, real or imaginary, to justify and defend their oppressive regimes. Conversely, it could be argued that even the more moderate regimes used the Cold War to justify certain policies and weapon programmes.

Until August 1957 Europe could safely 'sit' under the 'American nuclear umbrella', where the Americans convinced the Russians that any level of attack would result in massive nuclear retaliation. Things got a little more complicated at that time when the Russians successfully launched the world's first intercontinental ballistic missile (ICBM) and two months later, on 4 October, launched the first Earth-orbiting satellite, Sputnik. To complicate matters further, a little later they reached nuclear parity. This left the Americans with basically two choices: surrender or face annihilation. In response American policy makers looked to Europe to do more in its own defence and introduced various strategies to achieve this.

America has maintained substantial forces in Britain since the Second World War and this has done little to allay people's apprehensions. In July 1948, the first American deployment began with the stationing of B-29 bombers. The radar facility at RAF Fylingdales is part of the American

Ballistic Missile Early Warning System, the base is operated entirely by British personnel and has only one USAF representative, mainly for administrative purposes. Several other British bases have a significant American presence including RAF Croughton, RAF Alconbury and RAF Fairford. British military forces also deployed American tactical nuclear weapons under a NATO nuclear sharing policy. These included nuclear artillery, nuclear demolition mines and warheads for Corporal and Lance missiles deployed in Germany. The RAF also deployed American nuclear weapons – the Mark 101 nuclear depth bomb on Shackleton maritime patrol aircraft. Later this was replaced by the B-57, which was deployed on RAF Nimrod aircraft. These arrangements stopped in 1992. Britain also allowed America to deploy nuclear weapons from its territory, the first having arrived in 1954. During the 1980s nuclear-armed USAF Ground Launched Cruise Missiles were installed at RAF Greenham Common and RAF Molesworth. Nuclear bombs were also stored at RAF Lakenheath for deployment by based USAF F-15E aircraft. During the Cold War, critics of the special relationship jocularly referred to the United Kingdom as the biggest aircraft carrier in the world. Britain and America also jointly operated a military base on the Indian Ocean island of Diego Garcia and on Ascension Island, a dependency of Saint Helena in the Atlantic Ocean. During this period, the United States Strategic Air Command (SAC) kept 30 per cent of its nuclear armed bombers on alert, their crews ready to take off within fifteen minutes. In the early 1960s, during periods of increased tension, B-52s were kept airborne all the time and this practice continued until 1990.

Throughout this period Britain's nuclear policy was based on nuclear interdependence with America, although British political leaders often referred to this, and certainly tried to sell it to the public, as independence. Operational control of the Polaris force was assigned to Supreme Allied Commander Atlantic (SACLANT) and, like the V bomber force, targeting policy was determined by NATO's Supreme Allied Commander Europe (SACEUR). At times when the missiles would be launched without Britain's NATO allies, the independent targeting policy would apply. This relied on the 'Moscow criterion', basically Britain's capacity to retaliate against the centralised command structures concentrated in the Moscow area. In 1980, US President Jimmy Carter changed the original American MAD doctrine in by adopting a 'countervailing' strategy under which the planned response to a Soviet attack was no longer to bomb Soviet population centres and cities, but first to kill the Soviet leadership, then attack military targets, in the hope of a Soviet surrender before total destruction of the Soviet Union. This policy was further developed by the Reagan administration with the announcement of the Strategic Defense Initiative (nicknamed 'Star Wars') that aimed to develop a space-based technology to destroy Russian missiles before they reached America.

Events don't happen in isolation, they are all interconnected, like interwoven threads. They are twisted by people's interpretation of these events, which are influenced by their own aims, often their own personal aims, and perhaps with an eye to the future and how they want history to remember them. At the end of the day all we can be sure of is what happened, and this book tells the incredible story of the British Polaris project, which by any measure is a truly epic story and a truly a remarkable achievement. It stands alone as an example of managerial, logistical and leadership competency, both in its planning and execution, that even some sixty years later has not been equalled. Not only did the team procure a completely new major weapon system but it designed and built the submarines to carry them, constructed the two sizeable bases to support these submarines and their weapons and provided the correctly trained personnel to man them. Once the submarines became operational between 15 June 1968 and 15 May 1996, the four Polaris submarines of the 10th Submarine Flotilla carried out a total of 229 operational patrols, ensuring the British Continuous At Sea Deterrent (CASD) was ready at all times.

To try to put the Polaris project in context, Chapters 1 and 2 detail Cold War history and the British nuclear weapon programme, admittedly somewhat briefly but I hope it gives readers an overview of the background to the project. Being a Royal Navy project with more than a smattering of American input, acronyms abound. I have purposely avoided including a glossary and I explain the abbreviations in the text, avoiding the need for the reader to flip backwards and forwards through the book. For a similar reason, I have not included footnotes or references. If readers require further information, they should refer to the texts in the bibliography.

This is a story that I and my family were a part of; admittedly a small part but, as I'm sure it was for many others involved in the Polaris project, it was an enjoyable part and, I felt, a well worthwhile one. I also hope it is a story you will enjoy.

1

IN THE BEGINNING

Winston Churchill, the British Prime Minister, felt that a general election should be held as soon as possible after the Second World War ended; not to do so, he believed, would be a very serious constitutional failure and the majority of his party agreed with him. However, when the war ended in Europe on 8 May 1945 he reconsidered his decision and proposed to Attlee, the Labour Party Leader, that the election should be delayed until the Japanese had been defeated. Many Labour ministers in the Coalition agreed with his reasoning, although Herbert Morrison, the Home Secretary, did not. This proposal was put to the Labour party conference on 20 May 1945 and was overwhelmingly rejected; they wanted the election to be held sooner, despite Attlee wanting the election delayed until October. He argued that it would be impossible to compile an accurate register of voters any earlier. Atlee's decision was undoubtedly motivated by the fact that, the sooner the election was held the more the Conservatives would benefit from Churchill's respected position as the country's wartime leader. Probably as a result of this, Churchill called for an election much earlier than Labour had wanted. He resigned as leader of the Coalition government on 23 May 1945 and agreed to form what became known as the 'Caretaker Government' until the dissolution of Parliament, a few months later, on 15 June 1945.

Regrettably for the Conservatives their election campaign depended, almost entirely, upon Churchill's personal popularity; in fact, their manifesto was initialled 'Mr Churchill's Declaration of Policy to the Electors'. It high-lighted five areas that the Conservatives considered essential if the country was to recover from its post–war desolate state. They were: completing the war against Japan, demobilisation, restarting industry, rebuilding exports and a four-year plan regarding food, work and homes. Unfortunately it totally failed to address the people's concerns and priorities. On the other hand, the Labour Party manifesto detailed a wide-ranging set of proposals for the rebuilding of the devastated post-war Britain. Their plan proposed a programme of nationalisation that included: the Bank of England, fuel and power, inland transport and iron and steel. It also proposed that there should be controls on raw materials and food prices, government intervention to maintain employment, a National Health Service, social security, and controls on where industries should be located. This was much more in keeping with the voters' priorities. Housing, the last consideration for the Conservatives, was the overwhelming top priority for the voters, along with jobs, social security and nationalisation. Not surprisingly, Labour won a landslide victory – 393 seats to the Conservatives' 213.

Regrettably, the cost of the war shone the cold light of reality on these optimistic dreams. Although the actual costs were unknown, the war placed a colossal strain on the country's finances; it was estimated that approximately one quarter of the nation's wealth, some £7 billion, was spent on the war effort and the national debt had tripled. The leading British economist, John Maynard Keynes, who at the time was the chief economic advisor to the Labour Government, warned that the country was living well beyond its means and he thought that the country would not be able to enjoy its pre-war, world power position. He estimated the overspend to be in the region of some £2 billion a year. He stressed that without the lend-lease agreement with the US it was doubtful that the country could have won the war and once this arrangement ceased the country's worldwide commitments would in all probability have to be reduced with the related loss of national prestige. To avoid this, Keynes estimated, the country would need a loan of $5 billion dollars and America was the only credible source for this. He thought that if this loan was unobtainable the country's future could be likened to a second-class power, which he equated to the present state of France. This was an intolerable situation for British politicians, who still imagined the country's world standing in its pre-war state.

During the war the Americans supplied Britain, Russia, China, France and other allied nations with war materials and food. This aid programme became known as lend-lease, in which a total of $50 billion (approximately $639 billion in today's money) worth of supplies was shipped to these countries.

Once this stopped, Clement Attlee sent Keynes to America to obtain this loan and much to his credit, despite his ill health, he managed to secure $3.75 billion. The Canadians also loaned C$1.25 billion and the country also received £2.4 billion from the European Recovery Programme (the Marshall Plan). Even with these loans, money was still very tight and the Government was forced to adopt other money-saving solutions. Attlee's government introduced import controls and continued the wartime practice of rationing food. In fact, it got worse and between 1947 and 1948 about half of consumer expenditure on food was rationed. Such staple foods as meat, cheese, eggs, fats and sugar were rationed; bread had been rationed in July 1946, followed by potatoes in November 1947. Rationing was slowly relaxed between late 1948 and 1954, but coal remained rationed until 1958. The Government also implemented defence cuts, which caused Herbert Morrison to express his concern in November 1949 by stating the country could be paying more than it could afford for an inadequate defence organisation. The government also reduced capital investment, affecting roads, railways and industry. As promised, Labour embarked on a massive programme of nationalisation, with approximately 20 per cent of the economy involved. On top of this, the government created the very expensive National Health Service.

Despite the loans and Labour's best efforts, by 1947 the country's economy was in crisis. At the TUC conference in 1948, the Labour chancellor Sir Stafford Cripps announced, 'There is only a certain sized cake. If a lot of people want a larger slice they can only get it by taking it from others.' He had already introduced a wage freeze in his austerity budget the year before. The government's problems were further compounded when the winter that year turned out to be one of the worst on record and the wheat harvest failed, adding to the rationing problems and further increasing difficulties with the country's food supply. In 1949 Britain was forced to devalue the pound, from US$4.03 to US$2.80.

And while all this was going on, unnoticed by most, the next war had already started, or perhaps more correctly, entered a new phase: the Cold War. It was a name given to the post-war tensions between America and its allies and the Russian-led countries. It was a peculiar war. A proxy war. The main participants never directly fought one another, but in one way or the other it was a war that affected the lives of most of the people in the world. It was a war without a clear-cut start and, despite the celebrations during 1991, it's a war that's probably still in progress.

Despite their common origin – both America and Russia were born from revolution – they developed very different ideologies and very different attitudes in their dealings with the rest of the world. In America the state had little influence over the day-to-day life of its citizens; the Constitution limited the state's power. In contrast, primarily due to the influence of Eastern Orthodoxy and rule of the Tsar, Russia was a bureaucratic, land-based power that saw its security in terms of the land it owned. Additionally, there were major differences in the attitudes regarding empire-building. The Americans, along with many other Western nations, were primarily seafaring nations, whose economies were largely trade-based, whereas Russia tended towards isolationism viewing anything outside its direct control with a degree of suspicion.

It seems unlikely that this conflict between the two superpowers could have even been prevented. During the war there was never any real relationship, it was more a union based on need and convenience and the seeds that would grow into the Cold War were probably sown well before the Second World War.

Britain, or the Kingdom of England as it was known then, first established relationships with Russia in 1553 when the English navigator Richard Chancellor sailed to Arkhangelsk. He returned to England but revisited Russia in 1595. The Muscovy Company, which had the monopoly of trade between the two countries until 1698, was formed this year. Relationships were further improved when Peter I visited England in 1697. During the 1720s Peter invited English engineers to St Petersburg, and this eventually led to the formation of a small but nevertheless important 'expat' community.

During the eighteenth century the two countries were allies as often as they were on opposing sides in the various European wars. During the War of Austrian Succession they were allies, but eight years later, during the Seven Years War, they were on opposite sides, although they never actually fought one another. The outbreak of the French Revolution caused the two countries to unite in a political alliance against French republicanism. Their invasion of the Netherlands in 1799, which ended in failure, concluded this agreement. The two countries fought in the 1807 Anglo–Russia War, but joined forces against Napoleon in the Napoleonic Wars (1803–15). Both countries became involved with the Ottoman Empire and intervened in the Greek War of Independence (1821–29). Despite the London Peace Treaty, problems with the Ottomans were never fully settled and this eventually led to the Crimean War (1853–56), which saw the British, French and Ottomans join forces against the Russians.

Britain's objective was to stop Russian expansion into Ottoman Turkey; they were particularly worried about the Russians gaining a Mediterranean port that would allow them to, possibly, control the recently opened Suez Canal. This was to be a recurring theme in the following years. Britain was also concerned about the closeness of the Tsar's territorially expanding empire in Central Asia to India. This caused a number of conflicts in Afghanistan, which became known as 'The Great Game', further increasing the tension between the two countries. For example, in 1885 the Russians invaded Afghan territory, this became known as the Panjdeh Incident. Conversely, the two countries saw fit to join forces in the Boxer Rebellion (1899–1901). In October 1905 Russian ships mistakenly fired on several British fishing boats in the North Sea. Preparations were made for war and a flotilla of submarines was dispatched to engage the enemy. They were subsequently recalled before any 'shots', or indeed torpedoes, were fired. Britain was not the only country to find itself in conflict with Russia during the nineteenth century; there were several conflicts between Russia and America all centred on the opening of East Asia to American trade, markets and influence.

In 1907 the Anglo–Russian Entente and the Anglo–Russian Convention made both countries part of the Triple Entente, which led them to form an alliance against Germany and its allies in the First World War.

Many countries including Britain, France, Japan, Canada and America supported the White Russians against the Bolsheviks during the 1918–20 Russian Civil War. The revolution involved two separate coups; in February and October 1917, but it took a further three years for Lenin to finally come to power. America landed troops in Siberia in 1918 to protect its interests; they also landed forces at Vladivostok and Arkhangelsk. This undoubtedly coloured Russian attitudes in their dealings with the Western world over the coming years and hardened their suspicions of it. After this period tensions between Russia and the West turned more ideological in nature.

In the First World War, America, Britain and Russia were allies from April 1917 until the Bolsheviks seized power in Russia in November 1917. In 1918, Lenin negotiated a separate peace deal with the Central Powers (the German, Austro–Hungarian and Ottoman Empires and the Kingdom of Bulgaria) at Brest-Litovsk. This further compounded American mistrust of the Russians, it also left the Western Allies to fight the Central Powers alone while allowing the Germans to deploy more troops to the Western Front.

When the First World War ended on 11 November 1918, the conditions and penalties to be imposed on the defeated Germany were detailed in the Treaty of Versailles, which was signed on 28 June 1919. Many thought that the terms of treaty were disproportionally severe on Germany and it undoubtedly laid the foundations for the Second World War. The German economy, severely impaired by the effects of the war and its subsequent defeat, was crippled by the attempt to pay the reparations stipulated by the allies. The German government printed money and this caused a dramatic rise in inflation; in 1914 the Mark stood at 4.2 to the dollar, by 1922 it was 190 to the dollar and by the end of that year it was 7600. Incredibly, by the end of 1923 a dollar was worth 630 billion marks, and a simple loaf of bread cost 140 billion marks. The treaty also changed many of the European countries' boundaries. Edward Mandell House, an American present at the treaty negotiations, commented, 'To create new boundaries is to create new troubles'; history has shown how true his insight turned out to be. The treaty also set up the League of Nations, the forerunner of the United Nations, the intention being that the organisation would act as an arbitrator in international disputes, hopefully thereby avoiding wars.

Russia became progressively isolated from the international community, which Lenin chose to interpret as his country being encircled by hostile capitalist countries. He saw diplomacy as a weapon to keep Russia's enemies divided and to this end he created the 'Soviet Comintern' (Communist International), whose primary aim was to spread the Russian radical message, by all available means including armed force, to the overthrow of the international bourgeoisie with the aim of creating an international Soviet republic. At this time, Russia was the most authoritarian society in the world. In common with most other revolutions whose aim is to free the working classes, the Bolshevik Revolution had the reverse effect. It concentrated power in the hands of the few and provided a platform to enable communism to be spread.

In the West this resulted in a period of intense anti-Communist feeling, particularly in America. This became known as the First Red Scare, lasting from 1917 to 1920, and it was mostly concerned with worker revolution and political radicalism. Many in America saw the Russian system as a threat. Differences between the political and economic systems; capitalism versus socialism, isolationism versus trade, state planning versus private enterprise, were simplified and developed in national ideologies to differentiate two ways of life. The atheistic nature of Russian communism also concerned many Americans. These differences were further amplified by Woodrow Wilson's fourteen-point plan, which was an attempt to ensure there would be a better future for the world after the colossal loss of life that resulted from the war. Lenin's response, his Peace Decree, only underlined and highlighted the differences between the two countries.

At the end of the First World War the British Government and the fledgling trade union movement disagreed on several issues, not least of which was what the relationship should be with Russia. While the Conservative government was refusing to have any contact with Russia, the Labour Prime Minister Ramsay MacDonald had signed several agreements with the country and he was in favour of establishing formal relations. MacDonald also proposed that the Russians should be given a large loan. Because of these actions there were claims from the opposition benches that the government had been infiltrated by many communist sympathisers and agents. It appeared that Parliament would reject MacDonald's proposals and as a result the Prime Minister called a general election. Any hopes of a Labour victory were crushed when a letter, allegedly written by Zinoviev (head of the Comintern) was sent to the British Communist Party. It seemed to suggest that MacDonald's proposals would be useful for both the British and Russian Communist Parties and, more damning still, it went on to suggest that the British workers, with the help of the military, should rise up against the government. In response, MacDonald replied, stating his disapproval, but despite this, he lost the election.

During this period many European countries embarked on a variety of alliances and non-aggression pacts, all in the hope of counteracting the Germans and Russians and their hostile ideologies.

Joseph Stalin became Russian leader after Lenin's death on 21 January 1924. He regarded his country as a socialist island and he felt he had to fight capitalism and spread his socialist message throughout the world. He saw international politics to be, essentially, a two-part process; the East and the West. Countries that were attracted to socialism would naturally be drawn to Russia, on the other hand, Western countries would be drawn towards capitalism. Needless to say, fear and mistrust grew between the West and Russia, and this was driven by several events, primarily the Bolsheviks' challenge to capitalism; in 1926 the Russians helped fund the British general workers' strike. A consequence of this was that Britain broke off relations with

Russia, and matters were not improved when in 1927 Stalin announced that peaceful coexistence with 'the capitalist countries is receding into the past'; Russia claimed French and British involvement in a coup d'état during the Shakhty show trial, while more than half a million Soviets were executed during the Great Purge. During the 'Moscow show trials' it was implied that Britain, France, Japan and Germany were involved in espionage against Russia. Other things that affected Russia's relationship with the West included the death of 6–8 million people in the Ukrainian Soviet Socialist Republic in the 1932–33 famine, Western support of the White Army in the Russian Civil War, America's refusal to recognise the Soviet Union until 1933 and the Soviet entry into the Treaty of Rapallo. The latter was an agreement Russia and Germany signed on 16 April 1922 that committed each country to renounce all territorial and financial claims against the other following the Treaty of Brest-Litovsk and the First World War. The countries also decided to normalise diplomatic relations and to 'co-operate in a spirit of mutual goodwill in meeting the economic needs of both countries'. Just before the Second World War, as a result of Western appeasement of Adolf Hitler, the Russians arranged a series of meetings with the British and French in the hope of forming an alliance to counter the threat posed by Nazi Germany. This failed primarily due to British and French concerns regarding Bolshevism and socialist revolution.

Relationships between Russia and the West were even further damaged when, just one week before the outbreak of the Second World War, Russia signed a non-aggression pact with Germany, the Molotov–Ribbentrop Pact; named after the two foreign secretaries involved. This included a secret agreement to split Poland and Eastern Europe between the two states. One week later, in September 1939, the German and Russian armies invaded Poland. For the next eighteen months the two countries were involved in a wide-ranging economic relationship, including trading vital war materials. The Russians even permitted the basing of a submarine depot ship near the Kola Peninsula and went so far as to supply an ice-breaker, enabling a German commerce raider to break out into the Pacific Ocean. Stalin also stated that the Russians would not see Germany defeated and would offer direct military aid if required.

Although he probably did not mention to them at the time, Hitler thought the Russians were sub-human and Germany broke the Molotov–Ribbentrop Pact on 23 June 1941 with Operation Barbarossa; the invasion of

Russia through the territories that the two countries had previously divided between themselves. There is no such thing as a good war but the Russian conflict was unbelievably vicious and barbaric with a degree of vindictiveness that was almost primitive in its nature. Russia was devastated; more than 20 million Russian citizens died during the war, thousands of cities, towns and villages were destroyed, and 30,100 Soviet factories were wrecked.

Following the German invasion the Russians and their soon-to-be Western allies had little choice but to put aside their long history of mutual distrust and suspicion and to work together. The Americans shipped huge quantities of lend-lease material to the Russians and Britain signed a formal alliance with the Russians; the Americans did not join until after the attack on Pearl Harbour on 7 December 1941. Goods to Russia were carried in convoys that initially sailed from Iceland to Arkhangelsk or Murmansk, when winter ice closed Arkhangelsk. Cargo included tanks, fighter planes, fuel, ammunition, raw materials and food. The convoys were routed around occupied Norway and were subjected to German air, submarine and surface forces attack.

Both America and Russia entered the Second World War as a result of a surprise attack, but despite their common enemy there were disagreements on military tactics, especially the question of the opening of a second front against Germany in Western Europe. As early as July 1941, Stalin had asked Britain to invade northern France, but the country was in no position to carry out his request. The Russians believed at the time, and continued to claim throughout the Cold War, that the British and Americans intentionally delayed the opening of a second front against Germany in order to intervene only at the last minute, so as to influence the peace settlement and dominate Europe. They also felt that they were left to bear the brunt of the German assault, thereby weakening the Axis forces and making the eventual Allied invasion easier. Whatever the rationale behind the timing of the invasion, it added to the already existing atmosphere of tension and hostility between the Allied powers.

The Allies held a series of meetings during the war, initially to discuss strategy and latterly to determine what would happen at the end of the conflict. The first three meetings were primarily concerned with the conduct of the war. The final three meetings, if not intentionally laying the foundations for the post-war unrest between the Allies, certainly intensified existing misgivings and uncertainties and deepened the fundamental suspicions between

Russia and the West. Each of the leaders had his own agenda; Roosevelt wanted Russian support in the war against Japan, specifically help in invading Japan, Churchill pressed for free elections and democratic governments in Eastern Europe (specifically Poland) and Stalin demanded a sphere of political influence in Eastern Europe, arguing it was essential to Russian national security.

The first of the final three meetings was held in Tehran between 28 November and 1 December 1943. The aim of this meeting was to determine the final strategy for the war against Germany and set the date for Operation Overlord. Stalin took the opportunity to express concern that the Western Allies had not opened a second front in Western Europe.

The second meeting, between 4 and 11 February 1945, was held at Yalta on the Black Sea and was elemental in shaping Europe's balance of power in the post-war years. It was proposed that the defeated Germany should be divided into three zones; each one being occupied by one of the Allies. France was later granted a zone formed from relinquished parts of the American and Britain sectors. Berlin was in the Russian zone but it was agreed that it would be divided into three sectors, again with one of the Allies occupying each one. They also stated that all original governments would be restored to the invaded countries, with the exception of the French government, which they regarded as collaborationist. Stalin demanded that the Polish government-in-exile should be excluded. They also agreed that all civilians would be repatriated. They discussed a Russian request for reparations totalling $10 billion, which the Russians felt should be the basis for negotiations; this was agreed.

The third conference was held at Potsdam Germany from 17 July to 2 August 1945. Harry S. Truman, who became President on Roosevelt's death on 12 April 1945, represented America. Truman and his advisers took a harder line with the Russians than Roosevelt had done and tended to ignore officials who recommended collaboration with them. Britain was represented by Clement Attlee, who had replaced Churchill as Prime Minister after the Labour Party's victory in the recent general election. At Yalta, the Russians had demanded large post-war reparations from Germany. While Roosevelt had agreed to these demands, Truman and his Secretary of State, James Byrnes, were determined that occupying powers should only extract reparations from their own zone. The Americans adopted this position in the hope that it would avoid the situation created by the Treaty of Versailles, which had exacted high reparation payments from Germany following the First World War. The Allies also discussed the revision of the German–Russian–Polish borders and the expulsion of several million Germans from the disputed territories. Because of the land it lost to Russia, Poland received a large strip of German territory and it immediately began to deport the German residents, as did other countries that were host to large German minority populations. Although the Allies were well aware of this they did little to control the situation.

During the conference Truman informed Stalin that America had just detonated the first atomic bomb on 16 July 1945. Perhaps Truman was hoping to use this as a bargaining tool to temper some of the Russian leader's more extreme demands, but Stalin was more than well informed about the American nuclear programme and felt little need to reform his position. Finally, the Allies released the Potsdam Declaration, which threatened Japan with 'prompt and utter destruction' if it did not immediately surrender. As Russia was not at war with Japan it did not sign the declaration. This was to be the final conference of the war. The leaders of the three allied nations, who, despite their differences, had remained united throughout the war, would never again meet jointly to discuss cooperation in post-war reconstruction. The majority of the post-war arguments between American and Russian leaders were due to their contradictory perceptions of the outcomes of these conferences; not least of these were misunderstandings about the post-war Polish borders. One week after this conference nuclear bombs were dropped on Hiroshima and Nagasaki.

Before the war ended it became evident that collaboration between the Allies would, at best, be limited. It was even felt that there was a possibility that the alliance would totally break down and the Allies might even go to war against one another. Stalin thought that the Western nations would return to their rivalry over colonies and trade, giving Russia the opportunity to continue its expansionist ambitions. Eugen Varga, a Russian economic advisor, expected that the Americans would cut military spending, thereby causing serious problems of overproduction, which he believed would result in another depression. Stalin assumed, based on this advice, the Americans would offer the Russians aid in post-war reconstruction, primarily because they would need markets to sustain the industrial production that had greatly increased during the war. In the event, America's capital investments in industry were sustained and the predicted post-war crisis of overproduction was avoided. When Germany surrendered, the Americans ended lend-lease to the Russians; Moscow thought this showed that America had no intention to support it any more than it had to and this once again added to the mistrust.

At the end of the war the Russians occupied Eastern Europe, while the Allies had much of Western Europe. In occupied Germany the Americans and the Russians established the occupation zones as agreed at Yalta. Despite the assurances given at the Yalta Conference, Russia was attempting to create a 'puppet' state in the Caucasus (northern Iran). It was also threatening Turkey in an attempt to gain access to the Bosphorus river for the Russian Navy; it had moved into the Balkans, supporting communist parties in Yugoslavia, Albania and Greece and installing puppet governments in Romania and Bulgaria. Russia had also advanced into Poland, Hungary, Czechoslovakia and the eastern region of Germany, as was agreed at the Yalta Conference.

Stalin was determined to gain control of Poland and the Balkans and once and for all to destroy Germany's ability to wage war. On the other hand, the Americans saw a strong Germany as essential to the recovery of Europe and there was opposition to Russian domination over the buffer states. This fuelled fears that Russia was attempting to build an empire that would become a risk to the recovering European countries. Churchill was worried that the Americans would revert to pre-war isolationism; President Roosevelt had stated at Yalta that after the defeat of Germany all Americans would be withdrawn from Europe within two years. However, this would leave an exhausted Europe unable to defend itself against Russia.

Churchill was so worried about Russian intentions that in April–May 1945 the British War Cabinet's Joint Planning Staff Committee developed Operation Unthinkable; a plan 'to impose upon Russia the will of the United States and the British'. Essentially America and Britain would continue fighting, although now the adversary would be Russia. Understandably there was little appetite to continue the conflict.

In view of the Russians' aggressive strategy, the Americans had little option other than to react. Initially this resulted in the Truman Doctrine, which was, essentially, a policy of containment; the Americans would give support to countries that were attempting to resist communist takeover, be it by armed minorities or from outside pressure. This was followed by the Marshall Plan, which was also known as the European Recovery Programme (ERP). The American Secretary of State, George Marshall, proposed that loans would be provided to assist reconstruction and economic recovery in the devastated European states. Undoubtedly they were overriding humanitarian considerations in the general proposal; he was deeply moved by the sights he saw in post-war Europe, and in 1953 he was awarded the Nobel Peace Prize. Apart from developing the post-war Europe as a potential market for American companies it was hoped that the financial aid would stop certain European governments adopting communist policies.

Marshall's policy undoubtedly achieved its aims. Billions of dollars in economic and military aid were supplied to Western Europe, Greece and Turkey. The Greek military won its civil war and the Italian Christian Democrats defeated the powerful Communist–Socialist alliance in the elections of 1948. As the Marshall plan was not available to communist countries, the Russians proposed their own version, which was intended to promote trade within Eastern Europe, and this became known as the Molotov Plan.

On 27 December 1945 the International Monetary Fund (IMF) was formally established, having been initially discussed at the United Nations Monetary and Financial Conference held at the Mount Washington Hotel in Bretton Woods, New Hampshire, in July 1944. The 730 delegates, from forty-four allied nations, agreed to assist in the reconstruction of the world's international payment system in the aftermath of the war. Apart from the IMF, the International Bank for Reconstruction and Development (IBRD) was also founded at this conference. Russia was not represented.

Apart from problems in Europe, on the world stage the British Government had many other events to deal with. Many of the countries that made up the British Empire had fought for Britain during the war and now wanted recompense. They also wanted their independence and many were granted it during this period. In the country as a whole, attitudes were changing and imperialistic views were no longer considered in vogue. Also, the Americans were putting pressure on Britain to disband the Empire.

In 1947, the British Government announced its desire to terminate the Mandate that was formally granted by the UN allowing it to govern Palestine. The United Nations General Assembly adopted a resolution recommending its partition into an Arab state, a Jewish state and the Special International Regime for the City of Jerusalem. The Jewish leadership accepted the proposal, but the Arab Higher Committee rejected it and a civil war began immediately. The establishment of the State of Israel was declared in 1948.

Furthermore, the Dutch and French were trying to restore their pre-war empire in Indonesia and Indo-China respectively, while the Malayan communists were trying to drive the British out of their country. Meanwhile, a civil war had broken out between the communists and nationalists in China. In December 1949 the new Chinese communist leader Mao Zedong visited Russia and this resulted in the Sino–Soviet treaty, which created a massive communist area that had the potential – or so it was thought in the West – to become a catalyst that could enable the spread of communism all over the world.

During 1946, while serving in Moscow, the American politician George F. Kennan wrote what became known as the 'Long Telegram' and in this he outlined what he believed were the Russian objectives. He argued that the Russians were motivated by deep-rooted imperialism and Marxist ideology; this caused them to be expansionist and paranoid, and as such they presented a threat to America and its Western allies. In July 1947, he further developed his views in an article 'The Sources of Soviet Conduct in Foreign Affairs'. So powerful were the arguments that Truman based his policy of containment on Keenan's interpretation of Russian intentions. Later in the year the Soviet Central Committee secretary Andrei Zhdanov declared that the Truman Doctrine was 'intended for accordance of the American help to all reactionary regimes that actively oppose democratic people, bearing an undisguised aggressive character'.

Tensions over Germany escalated after Truman refused to give the Russians reparations from West Germany's industrial plants. He rightly believed that it would inhibit Germany's economic recovery and the Western Allies felt a strong Germany was essential for European economic revival. In retaliation Stalin made the Russian sector of Germany a communist state. It was not until 1951 that the dismantling of West German industry was finally brought to an end, when the country agreed to place its heavy industry under the control of the European Coal and Steel Community, which in 1952 took over the role of the International Authority for the Ruhr.

During June 1948, as a result of the challenging differences between the two sides, the negotiations stalled and the Russians cut land access to Berlin. This prompted several American generals to suggest bombing Russian airfields or even putting armed troops on the railway trains that were supplying the city. General L. Clay, the American Military Governor in Germany, warned that if Berlin fell into Russian control, the rest of West Germany would follow suit. Fortuitously, the more extreme options were considered disproportionate and the city was supplied by air; between 26 June 1948 and 30 September 1950 more than 2 million tons of coal, food and other supplies were delivered by American and British aircraft in what became known as the Berlin Airlift. The Berlin Blockade was one of the first major international crises in this phase of the Cold War and set the tone of suspicion, distrust and cynicism that would come to govern the attitudes of the two superpowers in their dealings with one another over the coming decades.

On 17 March 1948, Belgium, the Netherlands, Luxembourg, France and Britain, signed the Treaty of Brussels, which established a military alliance that looked to the Americans to help it to counter the Russian threat. This agreement was ratified in the North Atlantic Treaty of 1949. The five original countries were joined by America, Portugal, Italy, Denmark, Norway, Iceland, and Canada.

The next conflict of the Cold War was the Korean War. This lasted from 25 June 1950 until a ceasefire on 27 July 1953; there has never been an actual signed peace agreement. Starting as a civil war between communist North Korea and the Republic of South Korea, it quickly mushroomed into a proxy war between the capitalist powers of America and its allies and the communist powers of the People's Republic of China and Russia. The war resulted in the death of 33,742 American soldiers, with 92,134 wounded and 80,000 posted as missing in action (MIA) or taken prisoner of war (POW). Although no actual figures have been given, it is estimated that 1 million to 1.4 million Korean and Chinese troops were killed or wounded, and 140,000 MIA or POW.

When Stalin died in 1953 it was hoped that relationships between America and Russia would improve. However, Khrushchev, an old-school communist, became leader in 1956 and he was determined not to see Russia's status as a superpower decreased. By the late 1950s, relations between the two had deteriorated, partly due to the Hungarian uprising and the somewhat disturbing fact that Khrushchev frequently threatened the total nuclear annihilation of America and its allies. He asserted that he could obliterate any American or European city he chose. In spite of this, unlike his predecessor, he didn't believe in the inevitability of a war between the superpowers; he felt the two systems should live in peaceful coexistence. Behind his seemingly relaxed attitude was the belief that the Western capitalist system would collapse under its own greed and materialism, without any Russian help.

While strictly not a Cold War confrontation, the two superpowers become involved in the Suez Crisis; for the two major nations involved this was to radically alter their status in the world. The crisis started on 29 October 1956 with a military attack on Egypt by Britain, France, and Israel. The action came after Egypt decided on 26 July 1956 to nationalise the Suez Canal after the withdrawal of an offer by Britain and the United States to fund the building of the Aswan Dam. Undoubtedly the military operation was very successful but the political ramifications were catastrophic, particularly for Britain. Russia threatened to become involved, and the Americans demanded a ceasefire and sponsored resolutions in the UN Security Council calling for an end to hostilities, in an attempt to stop the conflict escalating. The British Government and the pound came under pressure and a ceasefire was announced on 6 November 1956, France not being given prior warning of this decision. The Prime Minister, Anthony Eden, was forced to resign. General de Gaulle saw this incident and its aftermath as final proof, as if it was needed, that France could not rely on its supposed allies. As a result, in 1957 the French Government embarked on its own nuclear programme, known as 'Force de frappe', and in 1966 de Gaulle withdrew France from the integrated NATO military command. In Canada, the Suez Crisis contributed to the adoption of a new national flag; a flag where any indication of the country's past, as a colony of France and Britain, was removed. This incident marked the weakening of both Britain and France as global powers; conversely Nasser's status in the Arab world was enhanced.

Russia suffered a significant setback in 1956 when the Sino–Soviet alliance began to deteriorate. Mao had defended Stalin when Khrushchev attacked his legacy; he accused the Russian leader of having lost his revolutionary stance. Khrushchev made many attempts to restore the alliance, but Mao refused to change his views. This resulted in a prolonged propaganda war, which eventually led to a military confrontation in 1969.

In 1957 America announced cuts in her forces in Europe and reduced the Second Tactical Air Force Division by half. At the same time Duncan Sandys, the Secretary of State for Defence, was stressing Britain's nuclear independence and stating the V bomber force would get priority over the conventional forces that the country committed to NATO, and that these conventional forces would be cut. The Defence White Paper presented by Sandys that year abolished conscription and essentially committed the country to a nuclear-based defence. This was to be Blue Streak, a nuclear missile weapon system totally controlled by Britain and armed with British warheads. Randolph Churchill, addressing the American Chamber of Commerce in November 1957, stated that RAF V bombers could destroy twelve cities in the region of Stalingrad and Moscow flying from their bases in Britain and Cyprus. He worryingly pointed out that Britain did not have that power at the time of Suez, but was now a major power again.

During November 1958, Khrushchev made an unsuccessful attempt to turn Berlin into an independent, demilitarised 'free city'. He demanded that America, Britain, and France withdraw their troops from the sectors they occupied within six months; failure to do so would result in transfer of control of Western access rights to the East Germans. Earlier Khrushchev, never at a loss for a suitable merry witticism, told Chairman Mao that, 'Berlin is the testicles of the West. Every time I want to make the West scream, I squeeze on Berlin.' NATO formally rejected the ultimatum in mid December and Khrushchev withdrew it in return for a Geneva conference on the German question.

Communist Eastern European states, expecting to benefit from the new Russian regime, were soon disappointed. Khrushchev believed that if he allowed them too much freedom, they might break away and weaken the barrier against the capitalist West. Revolts against Russia in East Germany in 1953 and in Poland in 1956 had been ruthlessly put down. In 1956 Hungary also tried to break free; many Hungarians saw the change in Russian leadership as an opportunity to split from Russia. There were demonstrations and protests, the consequence of which was that Russia invaded Hungary in November 1956. The Russians could not back down over Hungary in case it encouraged other communist states in Eastern Europe to revolt. As a result, 30,000 were killed and 200,000 fled to the West. The new Prime Minister, Imre Nagy, was arrested and executed. His replacement, János Kádár, was a hard-line communist. The West could do nothing to aid the Hungarians, any attempt to intervene would have been interpreted as an act of war and neither the Americans nor the Russians could afford the risk of all-out nuclear conflict. As a result, relations between the two superpowers deteriorated even further.

During the 1960s, the nature of the tension between the two superpowers changed. The battle for men's minds was replaced by more physical objectives and the enmity between the two was based principally on geopolitical goals, with America and Russia attempting to influence many Third World countries. Russia tried to influence many of the recently decolonised countries while the Americans used the CIA to remove a string of unfriendly governments and to support Western-friendly ones. In 1953, as a result of this strategy, Iran's first democratically elected government, under Prime Minister Mohammad Mosaddegh, was removed, as was Guatemala's democratically elected President, Jacobo Árbenz Guzmán, a year later. Between 1954 and 1961, America sent economic aid and military advisors to stem the collapse of South Vietnam's pro-Western regime. In the 1960s, when Khrushchev attempted to establish ties with India and other neutral states in the area, the Chagos archipelago was secretly handed to America by Britain to use as a military base. Officially part of the British Indian Ocean Territory, the Chagos archipelago is made up of more than sixty islands, the largest of which is Diego Garcia. More than 1,800 Chagossians were forcibly removed, many being sent to Mauritius and the Seychelles, others were brought to the UK, and some were even sent to Switzerland.

A summit was arranged in Paris in May 1960 between Khrushchev, Eisenhower, de Gaulle and Harold Macmillan. It did little to improve relationships between the two superpowers when it was cancelled at very short notice after an American U-2 spy plane was shot down by a SAM-2 missile over the town of Sverdlovsk in the Ural Mountains. The pilot, Gary Powers, ejected and was subsequently captured. Perhaps not surprisingly, Khrushchev insisted on a full apology but Eisenhower refused, saying that it was his country's duty to protect itself from surprise attacks. Powers was released seventeen months later in a spy swap operation.

The most serious crisis of the Cold War occurred when the Russians sited nuclear missiles in Cuba. The American President, John F. Kennedy, responded by placing the island under a naval blockade and informed his NATO allies on 27 October 1962 that the situation was critical and that America might find it necessary to take whatever military action may be necessary to protect its interests and that of its allies. The world came very close to an all-out nuclear exchange, and after a very worrying period Kennedy secretly agreed to remove all missiles in Turkey on the border with Russia if Khrushchev removed all the missiles in Cuba. This was particularly embarrassing for Khrushchev as the removal of the American missiles had not been made public, and this gave the impression that the Russians were backing down in a situation of their own making. As a direct result of this incident a telephone link was set up between Moscow and Washington enabling direct communication between the two leaders in the hope that future issues could be addressed before they escalated. The aftermath of the crisis led to the first efforts in the nuclear arms race to reduce the number of nuclear weapons and improve relations, even though the Cold War's first arms control agreement, the Antarctic Treaty, had already come into force in 1961.

Khrushchev was ousted in 1964, primarily due to the Politburo's embarrassment at his handling of the Cuban crisis. Despite being accused of rudeness and incompetence, ruining Soviet agriculture and authorising the construction of the Berlin Wall, a very public condemnation of the Russian Communist system, he was permitted to retire peacefully. He was replaced by the former secretary of the Communist Party, Leonid Brezhnev.

Two years later, French President Charles de Gaulle withdrew France's armed forces from NATO and expelled the organisation's troops from France; he did not agree with the Western reliance on America for its defence against Russian aggression.

In Czechoslovakia during 1968, a period of political liberalisation that became known as the Prague Spring occurred. Press freedom was increased, as was freedom of speech and freedom of movement. Western policies such as an economic emphasis on consumer goods and multiparty government were considered, and the powers of the secret police were limited. The new government even suggested leaving the Warsaw Pact. This state of affairs was unacceptable to Russia and as a result armies from the Warsaw Pact led by Russia invaded Czechoslovakia in August 1968. This caused a wave of emigration, including an estimated 70,000 Czechs initially fleeing, with the total eventually reaching 300,000. The invasion generated strong protests from Yugoslavia, Romania and China, and Western European communist parties. One month after the Czechoslovakian invasion, Brezhnev outlined the Brezhnev Doctrine during a speech at the Fifth Congress of the Polish declared United Workers' Party. He stated he would violate the sovereignty of any country attempting to replace Marxism–Leninism with capitalism.

America maintained its support of friendly Third World regimes, particularly in Asia by pouring in vast amounts of money, most blatantly in Vietnam. America sent 575,000 troops to Southeast Asia in an attempt to defeat the National Front for the Liberation of South Vietnam (NLF). Unfortunately, this costly and very unpopular policy weakened the American economy and, by 1975, the Americans were forced to abandon Vietnam in what was seen as a humiliating defeat at the hands of one of the world's poorest nations.

America also supported South American dictators in their efforts to suppress leftist dissent in a campaign that became known as Operation Condor. The Americans assumed, not always correctly, that Russia or Cuba were backing these opposition movements.

The Russians supplied arms and economic aid to Egypt and, with some reluctance, assisted them in both the Six-Day War (1967) by supplying advisers and technicians and in the War of Attrition (1967–70), in which the Russians supplied both pilots and aircraft. Syria and Iraq also received assistance, and it was rumoured that the Palestinian Liberation Organisation (PLO) received support, although not directly. During the Yom Kippur War in 1973 it was thought that the Russians might intervene on the Egyptians' side and this sparked a massive American mobilisation. This was Russia's first intervention into a regional conflict that directly involved an American ally, and this episode heralded a much more volatile period in the superpower relationship, the Russians feeling more confident as they now had nuclear parity with the Americans.

The Americans were not exactly passive during this period. In 1969 American President Richard Nixon exploited the tension between China and Russia by visiting China, whilst the Chinese had tried to improve relations with the Americans in order to gain advantage over the Russians. In February 1972, Nixon met with Russian leaders, including Brezhnev, in Moscow. This meeting led to the first comprehensive nuclear weapon limitation treaty SALT 1 and the Anti-Ballistic Missile Treaty, which banned the development of systems designed to intercept incoming missiles. Nixon and Brezhnev announced an age of 'peaceful coexistence' and this new accord led to the policy of détente. Further collaboration took place between 1972 and 1974, when both countries agreed to strengthen economic ties and signed several trade deals.

In West Germany, Chancellor Willy Brandt introduced '*Ostpolitik*', a policy designed to stabilise its relationship with its Eastern European neighbours, particularly the German Democratic Republic. This and several other agreements led to the Helsinki Accords signed at the Conference on Security and Co-operation in 1975, which improved relationships between Western and Eastern European countries.

Despite détente, the superpowers continued to challenge one another indirectly throughout this period, particularly during the political crises in the Middle East, Chile, Ethiopia and Angola.

President Jimmy Carter attempted to negotiate another nuclear arms limitation agreement, SALT II, in 1979. Unfortunately world events deemed otherwise; pro-US regimes were ousted in Iran and Nicaragua, and approximately 75,000 Soviet troops invaded Afghanistan in order to support the Marxist government formed by ex-Prime Minister Nur Muhammad Taraki. As a result of this latter event, Carter withdrew the SALT II treaty and imposed embargoes on grain and technology shipments to Russia. He also requested an increase in military spending, and stated that America would boycott the 1980 Moscow summer Olympics. He described the Russian intervention in Afghanistan as 'the most serious threat to the peace since the Second World War'.

When Ronald Reagan became American President in 1980, he increased military spending, primarily in response to the perceived Russian threat. He had an ally in the recently elected British Prime Minister Margaret Thatcher; both had criticised the Russian ideology. Reagan considered Russia an 'evil empire' and predicted that communism would be left on the 'ash heap of history'. He also imposed economic sanctions on Poland in protest at the suppression of the Solidarity trade union. In response, Mikhail Suslov, the Kremlin's top ideologist, advised Russian leaders not to intervene if Poland fell under the control of Solidarity, for fear it might lead to heavy economic sanctions, which he felt would be a disaster for the country's economy. The Russian economy was particularly susceptible to economic sanctions, and the military accounted for a quarter of the country's gross national product. This spending led to the well-publicised lack of consumer goods and the endless queues, and it seriously limited the investment in the country's infrastructure, causing a decade of economic stagnation during the later Brezhnev years.

During this period, the Russian armed forces were the largest in the world, both in terms of the numbers and types of weapons they possessed and the number of personnel serving. Despite this numerical supremacy the Eastern Bloc lagged behind the West regarding technical issues, often by a large degree. Reagan restarted the B-1 Lancer (four-engine supersonic variable-sweep wing, jet-powered heavy strategic bomber) programme in the early 1980s; introduced the LGM-118 Peacekeeper (land-based ICBM); installed American cruise missiles in Europe, and announced the Strategic Defense Initiative, his 'Star Wars' programme, whose sole aim was to make missiles obsolete. The Russians did little to respond to the American military build-up other than deploying RSD-10 Pioneer ballistic missiles, which were targeted at Western Europe.

The enormous cost compounded by inefficient manufacturing and an unproductive and disorganised collectivised agriculture industry, which were already a heavy burden for the Russian economy, prevented them from responding to this build-up. Added to this, Reagan convinced Saudi Arabia to increase its oil production, despite non-OPEC nations increasing production at the same time. This caused the 1980s 'oil glut', which, with oil being the main source of Russian export revenues, caused further problems for the Russian economy.

On 1 September 1983, the Soviet Union shot down a Boeing 747; Korean Air Lines Flight 007, when it violated Soviet airspace just off the west coast of Sakhalin Island. All the 269 people on board were killed, among them Congressman Larry McDonald. Reagan referred to this act as a massacre.

Remembering the humiliation that resulted from the Vietnam War, the Reagan administration preferred the use of quick, low-cost, counter-insurgency tactics to intervene in foreign conflicts. In 1983, he intervened in the multi-sided Lebanese Civil War; invaded Grenada; bombed Libya and backed the Central American Contras, anti-communist paramilitaries seeking to overthrow the Soviet-aligned Sandinista government in Nicaragua. While Reagan's interventions against Grenada and Libya were popular in America, his backing of the Contra rebels was, at best, controversial.

The Russians did not fare much better, with their own foreign interventions sustaining both high costs and international disapproval. In 1979 Brezhnev was convinced Afghanistan intervention would be short, however Muslim guerrillas waged a ferocious fight against the Russians, aided by the Americans and several other Western countries. Some 100,000 Russian troops were sent to Afghanistan to support the puppet regime, in what became known as the Soviets' Vietnam, although the Russians fared much worse than the Americans had, an outcome that had been predicted by an American State Department Official in 1980.

The age and frailty of the Russian leaders did not help matters. Brezhnev, who was virtually incapacitated in his later years, was succeeded by Andropov and then Chernenko, both dying within a short time of one another. After Chernenko's death, when Reagan was asked why he had not negotiated with Russian leaders, he replied, 'They keep dying on me.'

In 1985 the comparatively youthful Mikhail Gorbachev became General Secretary. He inherited a stagnant economy where low oil prices had caused a sharp fall in foreign currency revenues. Gorbachev introduced several measures to remedy this. However, initially these did not work, and in June 1987 he instituted more radical structural changes that became known as *Perestroika*. This policy relaxed the production quota system, allowed private ownership of businesses and paved the way for foreign investment. His intention was to redirect the country's resources from the expensive Cold War military commitments to more profitable areas in the civilian sector. He proved to be committed to reversing Russia's declining economy, despite initial Western scepticism. At the same time he introduced *Glasnost*, which increased freedom of the press and the transparency of state institutions, which he hoped would reduce the corruption at the top of the Communist Party and moderate the abuse of power in the Central Committee. It also permitted contact between Russian people and the Western world, particularly with America; this provided a boost to the already accelerating process of détente between the two countries.

In response, Reagan agreed to renew talks on economic issues, collaboration and the possibility of reducing the number of nuclear arms each nation held. The first initial talks were held in November 1985 in Geneva, Switzerland. These were very positive and at one stage the two leaders, only accompanied by a translator, agreed in principle to reduce their nuclear arsenal by 50 per cent.

A second meeting was held at Reykjavík, Iceland, in October 1986. The talks were progressing well until the subject of the Strategic Defense Initiative was raised: Gorbachev wanted research into this project stopped, Reagan refused. Although these negotiations failed, a third summit was arranged in 1987 and this resulted in the signing of the Intermediate Range Nuclear Forces Treaty (INF). This removed all nuclear-armed, ground-launched ballistic and cruise missiles with ranges between 300 to 3,400 miles and their supporting infrastructure.

As tensions between East and West decreased throughout the mid to late 1980s, a final summit was held in Moscow, where Gorbachev and Reagan's successor, George H.W. Bush, essentially completed the talks started in Reykjavík and signed the START I arms control treaty.

The following year it became apparent that the oil and gas subsidies, and the cost of maintaining such large military forces, were representing a significant drain on the Soviet Union's financial reserves. Gorbachev also questioned the security advantage offered by the buffer zone made up of the communist Eastern European countries. He felt this arrangement had little to offer in the new political landscape and was largely irrelevant, so he declared that Russia would no longer intervene in the internal affairs of allied states in Eastern Europe. In 1989, Russian forces withdrew from Afghanistan and by 1990 Gorbachev had agreed to Germany's reunification. On 3 December 1989, Gorbachev and Reagan's successor, George H.W. Bush, had declared the Cold War over at the Malta Summit; a year later, they were allies in the Gulf War against long-time Russian ally, Iraq.

Strangely, Gorbachev's goodwill that he had shown towards Eastern Europe did not initially extend to his own territory. George Bush found it necessary to criticise the January 1991 killings in Latvia and Lithuania, despite his constant efforts to maintain friendly relations. He felt it necessary to warn Gorbachev that economic ties would be frozen if the violence continued.

By this time, the Soviet system had virtually broken down and now the Russian military could no longer support the Communist leaders of the Warsaw Pact states they lost power. *Glasnost* had undermined the bonds that held the Union together and led the different republics to declare their independence, with the Baltic states withdrawing completely. Across Central and Eastern Europe the old Soviet-style communist governments were overthrown, such as Poland, Hungary, Czechoslovakia and Bulgaria, Romania being the only Eastern Bloc country to topple its communist regime violently and execute its head of state. By February 1990, with the dissolution of the Soviet Union looming, the Communist Party was forced to surrender its 73-year-old monopoly on state power. Presidential elections, the first in the country's history, were held on 12 June 1991 and Boris Yeltsin was elected. As part of a backlash from communist hardliners there was a coup in Russia that August and its failure marked the end of the Soviet empire. Several Soviet republics, particularly Russia, threatened to separate from the USSR and the union was declared officially dissolved on 25 December 1991. Two days earlier, the Commonwealth of Independent States was introduced as a successor to the Soviet Union. Its intention was to facilitate a civilised break-up of various Soviet republics.

The most graphic symbol of the ending of the Cold War was the fall of the Berlin Wall, filmed and spread round the world; the final damning denunciation of the failings and shortcomings of the communist system. Considering what the wall stood for: the repression, the suffering, its whole dreadful history, its ending seemed almost comical.

The number of refugees leaving East Germany for the West had been increasing throughout this period. On 9 November, the Politburo, led by Egon Krenz, agreed to allow refugees to leave directly through the crossing points between East and West Germany, including those in West Berlin. On the same day, the ministerial administration modified the proposal to include private travel, and it was intended that these new regulations would come into force the next day. The SED Politburo party leader and spokesman in East Berlin, Gunter Schabowski, was due to announce the new arrangements. Unfortunately, he had not been involved in the discussions about the new rules and was not fully up to date on the latest developments. Just before the press conference was due to start, he was given a brief note detailing the changes. With little choice, he read the note out loud word for word, whereupon one of the reporters enquired when the new regulations would come into effect. Schabowski assumed it would be the same day based on the wording of the note and replied that as far he was aware the border should be opened immediately. Needless to say, this momentous statement was the lead story on West Germany's two main news programmes that night and this in turn meant that the news was broadcast to East Germany as well. Later that night, it was broadcast that East Germany had announced that the borders were open; it was a truly historic day.

After the broadcast, East Germans began to assemble at the wall and at the six checkpoints, insisting that the guards opened the gates immediately. The very worried guards were totally unprepared, they made frantic telephone calls to their superiors and were initially ordered to find the more aggressive protesters at the gates and stamp their passports so they could not return to East Germany. Despite this radical action there were still thousands of people demanding to be let through the border.

It became apparent, very quickly, that no one in authority would issue the order to use lethal force, so the border guards had little option but to open the checkpoints and, at 10.45 p.m., the guards finally opened the checkpoints and allowed the people through with little or no identity checking. Soon West and East Berliners jumped on top of the wall and, amid scenes of excited celebration, they began to demolish it.

Surprisingly, the fall of the Berlin Wall and what it signified was not universally welcome, and the thought of a reunified Germany caused concern in some quarters. In September 1989, British Prime Minister Margaret Thatcher pleaded with Russian President Mikhail Gorbachev not to let the Berlin Wall fall and confided that she wanted the Soviet leader to do what he could to stop it. She did not want to see a united Germany, which she felt would lead to a change to post-war borders. This, she felt, could undermine the stability of the whole international situation and potentially destabilise Europe's security. French President François Mitterrand warned Mrs Thatcher that a unified Germany could, possibly, be more threatening than Adolf Hitler had ever been and that Europe would have to bear the consequences.

These misgivings aside, it was time to take stock. Despite the celebrations and the talk of the expected peace dividend, the Cold War was not over, it merely moved into another phase and, if truth were told, a more unsettled and perhaps a more dangerous phase. Unbelievable amounts of time, effort and money had been spent by all the countries involved on military hardware and gathering intelligence. There was a significant reduction in Russian military spending, and, as one in five of Russian adults were employed in the military–industrial sector, millions became unemployed. The country's financial situation worsened after it embarked on capitalist economic reforms in the 1990s, resulting in a financial crisis and a recession. Military expenditure by America during the Cold War years was estimated to have been $8 trillion,

Unlike the wall, the legacy of the Cold War was not as simple to remove, and many of the economic and social tensions that were exploited to fuel East–West rivalry in parts of the Third World remained. The breakdown of state control in a number of areas formerly ruled by communist governments produced a series of civil and ethnic conflicts, particularly in the former Yugoslavia. In Eastern Europe, the end of the Cold War ushered in an era of economic growth and a large increase in the number of liberal democracies. Unfortunately, in other parts of the world, Afghanistan for example, independence was followed by state failure. After such an intense period of mutual mistrust and scepticism it was, at best, doubtful if the world would or indeed could 'return to normal', and the Cold War continues to influence global affairs. After the collapse of the Soviet Union, America was considered the sole remaining superpower; this is now being challenged by China and the re-emergence of Russia.

The underlying theme of the post-Second World War phase of the Cold War was the 'special relationship', a term used to describe the, seemingly, unusually close political, diplomatic and cultural relationship between Britain and America, which was strengthened by a shared language and an entwined history. While both countries maintained close relationships with many other countries, it is an unquestionable fact that the level of cooperation in the planning and execution of military operations, nuclear weapons technology and intelligence sharing with each other did not exist between other major world powers. Whether this relationship was the cosy liaison built on deep friendships and a shared culture and values depicted by some or a more hard-headed, self-centred business association is open to debate. The actual state of affairs is probably somewhere between the two and the goodwill and closeness of the relationship moved between the two extremes to suit the needs of either country at any particular time. In truth it was a relationship based more on self-interest, convenience and necessity rather than any feelings of goodwill and friendliness, particularly in the upper levels of government. That said, at lower levels of government and amongst members of the military there were many true and deep personal friendships. Other than military cooperation, there is a considerable amount of financial collaboration between the two countries. America is the largest source of foreign direct investment in the British economy, and Britain is the largest single investor in the American economy. British trade and capital have been important components of the American economy since its colonial inception. Until recently in trade and finance, the special relationship has been described as well-balanced, with London's light-touch financial regulation drawing a massive outflow of capital from New York.

During the Second World War Britain needed American help both militarily and in terms of material support if it was going to stand any chance of defeating Germany. Churchill, himself half-American, spent much time and effort cultivating the relationship that, while it greatly assisted the war effort, eventually cost Britain much of her wealth and ultimately her empire.

Before America entered the war this aid was delivered under an agreement called Cash and Carry, a policy introduced by President F.D. Roosevelt on 21 September 1939. It permitted the sale of material to warring nations as long as they transported it in their own ships and paid in cash before 'collecting' the goods. By adopting this approach, America hoped to remain neutral while helping Britain; Germany had no money and it would have had difficulty shipping the goods across the largely British-controlled Atlantic Ocean. Unfortunately for Britain, the one thing the Americans did not want was to be paid in sterling; they felt there was a very real possibility that if Britain was invaded by Germany it would render the British currency worthless. To overcome this problem the first payments were made by signing over British-owned businesses in America. After this, British gold was transferred to America from Canada; at the start of the war British gold reserves and securities were transferred by the Royal Navy to Canada (Operation Fish), while US Navy ships were dispatched to South Africa to collect British gold reserves.

So the 'special relationship' got off to a somewhat uneasy start, although Churchill did not actually use the term until 1945 when he used it to describe not only Britain's relationship with America, but to also to stress the country's close ties with Canada.

In November 1945 American President Harry Truman held a meeting on board USCG *Sequoia* with the British Prime Minister Clement Attlee and Mackenzie King of Canada to discuss the atomic bomb. During the meeting he stressed that in his opinion only an association of English-speaking peoples could prevent war and run the global organisations that would be necessary to achieve this.

Churchill used the phrase again in his 'Sinews of Peace Address' in Fulton, Missouri, on 5 March 1946, where he emphasised the special relationship between America and the English-speaking nations of the British Commonwealth. He also stressed the dangers of Russian expansion when he referred to an Iron Curtain descending across Europe.

The efficacy of the relationship often seems to have depended upon the personal relationship between the President and the Prime Minister. Particular highpoints include the relationships between Harold Macmillan – who, like Churchill, had an American mother – and John F. Kennedy, and between Margaret Thatcher and Ronald Reagan. Thatcher was of the opinion that the relationship had done more for the defence and future of freedom of the world than any other alliance. The empathy between the two was momentarily strained by Reagan's belated support in the Falklands War, but this was more than countered by the Anglophile American Defence Secretary, Casper Weinberger, who provided communications intercepts and approved shipments of the latest weapons to the massing British task force. Later, Thatcher was the only Western leader to allow American F-111s to take off from bases on her own soil prior to bombing Libya; she justified this by saying she was helping Reagan to 'turn the tide against terrorism'. On the eve of the war in Iraq, as Britain prepared to fight alongside America, Tony Blair spoke of the blood price that Britain should be prepared to pay in order to sustain the special relationship.

Low points have included Dwight D. Eisenhower's opposition to British involvement in Suez under Anthony Eden and Wilson's refusal to enter the war in Vietnam. Surprisingly, relations soured during the Thatcher period when the Americans invaded the Commonwealth island of Grenada, then went on to put Britain's nuclear deterrent at risk with the proposed Strategic Defense Initiative (Star Wars). Reagan's proposal, at the Reykjavík Summit, to eliminate all ballistic nuclear weapons, despite the large differences in conventional forces between East and West, did little to improve matters. Despite these disputes it was said that during this period Britain figured more prominently in American strategy than any other European power.

For a short period after the war America was the only country to possess the nuclear bomb, so it could easily counter any Russian aggression towards its Western allies and markets by threatening 'massive nuclear retaliation'. During the 1960s, with the Russians achieving nuclear parity by stockpiling weapons, the deterrence policy changed to one of Mutual Assured Destruction (MAD) and with the American withdrawal from Vietnam and the normalisation of relations with China, the policy of containment was gradually replaced by a new one of détente. This period was characterised by a general reduction in the tension between Russia and America; this lasted from the late 1960s until the start of the '80s. The original American MAD doctrine was modified on 25 July 1980, with President Jimmy Carter's adoption of a countervailing strategy under Presidential Directive 59. According to its architect, Secretary of Defense Harold Brown, the strategy stressed that the planned response to a Soviet attack was no longer to bomb Soviet population centres and cities primarily, but first to kill the Soviet leadership, then attack military targets, in the hope of a Soviet surrender before total destruction of the Soviet Union (and the United States). This modified version of MAD was seen as a winnable nuclear war, while still maintaining the possibility of assured destruction for at least one party. This policy was further developed by the Reagan administration with the announcement of the proposed development of the Strategic Defense Initiative. This 'space-based' technology was intended to destroy Russian Soviet missiles before they reached America, essentially rendering ballistic missiles redundant. Under Reagan there was also a build-up of conventional arms, partly due to concerns of growing Russian influence in Latin America.

To many Britons brought up on stories of how English-speaking democracies rallied around their country in the Second World War, the special relationship is something to treasure. As Churchill pointed out, it was a bond forged in battle. The Americans do not see it in quite the same emotionally charged way, and US politicians are positively unrestrained with the use of the term, declaring their 'special relationships' with, Israel, Germany and South Korea, among others.

Although Britain is often viewed as the junior partner in the special relationship, both countries used it to achieve or further their own, often widely differing, aims. However, there was one common aim; once the Second World War ended it became patently obvious that the devastated European countries could not defend themselves against any future Russian aggression; be that physical or the Russians sponsoring communist-leaning governments in certain European countries. As Britain's security was inextricably linked to that of Europe, it was crucial that America remained involved in Europe as it was the only country that could present a credible defence against any Russian threat. This was no mean feat, prior to the Second World War Anglo–American relations had been somewhat frosty and towards the end of the war the Americans made it very clear that they intended to withdraw all their troops from Europe within two years of the war ending. It was a remarkable achievement that Britain managed to maintain American commitment to post-war Europe, especially in view of its isolation of the inter-war period. A senior British diplomat in Moscow, Thomas Brimelow, pointed out that it was Britain's capacity to get others to do our fighting that unsettled the Russians most; they respect Britain's ability to collect friends. He also remarked that the success or failure of American foreign economic peace aims depended, almost entirely, on its cooperation with Great Britain. It could also be argued that the American decision to stay involved in Europe was in keeping with the Truman Doctrine as there were several potential communist governments in Europe. Also, perhaps a little cynically, the Americans were defending their investment and potential markets; after the war the US was the only country that could supply the goods Europe needed; in fact 70 per cent of Marshall Aid was spent in America on American goods and services.

The First Sea Lord meeting Resident Officer Polaris Executive in the mid 1960s. (Open Government Licence v3.0)

HMS *Wakeful*. She was used as a tender to the 10th Submarine Squadron, and carried out a variety of duties, including acting as a target! (Open Government Licence v3.0)

HMS *Repulse* returning from her first deterrent patrol. (Open Government Licence v3.0)

AFD 60 leaving Faslane.

HMS *Resolution*. (Open Government Licence v3.0)

A Polaris missile second–stage test. (Open Government Licence v3.0)

SUBMARINERS 'CAPTURE' SATELLITE LANES

Blimey, the British Have Arrived!

The Fleet's in, mates, and it looks as though the Gallery Lounge at the Satellite Lanes is under martial law. The British aren't coming; they've arrived.

The HMS Resolution, one of the world's largest nuclear submarines, is berthed at Port Canaveral and the British sailors have lost no time in seeking B.A.D. nightlife.

How they ever strayed as far south as Satellite Beach is a mystery, but the word is out and Her Majesty's submariners have adopted the Gallery Lounge.

"They've been here all week; it's wild, man," says organ player **Barry Wayne...**

I've never sold so much beer in one week in my life," says bartender **Paul Moore.** And it looks like enough pitchers of beer are being consumed to float the MHS Resolution, yet the submariners remain quiet, courteous and charming. Their only complaint is that the beer's too cold, so they let it sit for a while until it warms up.

According to Chief Rod "Father" Frostick, "As far as the British are concerned, this is the greatest place in town."

Many of the sailors hitchhike to Satellite Beach, but some of them are lucky enough to find an American benefactor like Danny Kuhn, a Patrick Air Force-type, who makes the trip to the port to drive some of the lads south.

Like most entertainers with a responsive audience, Wayne is knocking himself out to put on a good show for the visiting British seamen and they thoroughly enjoy it. Some of the sailors cheering on his antics Wednesday night were **Dave Freke, Terry Nash, Guy Blackhead, Ted Burton** (no, no relation to Richard), **Ray Meyer** (an American submariner), **Richard Evans** and **David Bole.** The latter two informed B.A.D. that this was their second American port, the first being Charleston. They were sorely disappointed with Charleston — "We expected to see skyscrapers."

Not to be completely overpowered by the British **Myron** and **Louise Cross** entertained several sailors off the American destroyer, the USS Fred T. Berry, which also is in port. They included **Paul Deegan, Miachael Martin** and **Gene Jack.**

Barry Wayne and Paul Moore expect a busy weekend and if the crowd warrants it, they'll open up the huge back room at the lanes on Saturday night.

Blimey, it should be a jolly good show!

B.A.D. PEOPLE: Marge Carr and Jim Gardner listening to Johnny Bolan Trio at the Carnival

Lounge . . . Steve Gibbs has added a harpsichord to his instruments at the Sheraton Cape Colony . . . Among those making the scene at Mark Wayne's opening were **Lowell** and **Bobbi Fenner, Roger** and **Evelyn Graefe** of George's Fine Foods, **Kenny** and **Felice Baliss , Gene Sheldon** of The Illusions currently playing at the Starw Hat Club, **Jerry** and **Dee Maak** celebrating their fourth wedding anniversary and **Mrs.** and **Mrs. Wendell Ruck** celebrating their 24th wedding anniversary.

Following a party at Guilloteen's drummer **Joe Davis'** apartment at Palms East, **Hal Martin, Charlie Clendennen, Ann Lindecamp, Fred Hartman..** and **Nancy Condes** made the rounds and wound up at Mac's Zoo Room in Melbourne.

NIGHT CRAWLERS: Tom Andrews and **Anne Sier** enjoying dinner at Indialantic's Treasure Coast and catching the Peggy Lloyd — George Shaw act . . . **Dave Lilies,** guitar player with the Sharpshooters, returns to the stage next week after recovering from an operation.

DESPERATION RIDDLE: What goes 99-thump-thump, 99-thump-thump? A centipede with a wooden leg. And that's not only B.A.D., it's down right T.E.R.R.I.B.L.E.

A local newspaper report of HMS *Resolution*'s first commission DASO.

A view of the control room, looking forwards. (Open Government License v3.0)

The Commissioning by

The Port and Starboard Crews

OF

H.M.S. RESOLUTION

UNDER THE COMMAND OF

COMMANDER M. C. HENRY, ROYAL NAVY (PORT)

AND

COMMANDER K. D. FREWER, ROYAL NAVY (STARBOARD)

at Barrow-in-Furness

on Monday, 2nd October, 1967

*

Service of Blessing conducted by

THE RIGHT REVEREND THE LORD BISHOP OF BUCKINGHAM

THE RIGHT REVEREND MGR. G. E. PITT, C.B.E., ROYAL NAVY

THE REVEREND R. G. WILLIAMS, C.B.E., Q.H.C., ROYAL NAVY

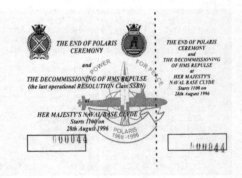

Above: A ticket for the End of Polaris Ceremony held in the shiplift at Faslane on 28 August 1996.

Left: HMS *Resolution*'s commissioning service. (Open Government Licence v3.0)

Editorials

TODAY

James Head
Executive Editor

Jack Breibart
Managing Editor

Fred Andersen
Associate Editor

Bully for HMS Resolution

Officers and crews of HMS Resolution have made an excellent impression on observers in and around the Cape Kennedy and Cocoa Beach areas the past several days.

Main reason was the dispatch with which they carried out their perfect first launch of a Polaris missile 40 miles at sea.

The Resolution has two crews. They are equal. Neither is what our NASA or Air Force people term "prime."

While one crew was carrying out the firing, the other watched with critical eye from the U.S. destroyer Fred T. Berry and muttered to anyone who would listen, "We can do better than that."

Which is a fine example of the team spirit which results from an all volunteer roster in the armed forces, as Britain has.

Both officers and men have become instant favorites at various Cocoa Beach spots they have visited since their arrival. One manager told a TODAY reporter, "They are gentlemen, all of them. They take care of themselves and, when necessary, of each other."

There is quite a story behind the kilt swirling bagpiper who tromped the missile deck of the Resolution after the perfect firing. Lance Corporal David Cairns is now a full-fledged member of the crew, but only

a few weeks ago he was driving a tank for the Scotch Greys.

His presence was a strong reminder the Scotch people were not being heard almost a decade ago when the first American Polaris subs docked in their country. Professional agitators from England led the protest marchers when the subs with their atomic warheads arrived.

Three more missile-firing submarines are now in the building ways and within the next two years will join the Resolution as part of Britain's contribution to NATO.

All will be coming to the Cape Kennedy waters for test launches before getting full credentials for patrol duty.

Any professional bleeding heart who tried to storm the Cape Kennedy gates and put on a demonstration akin to the one in Scotland in the early 1960s would never make it past the guards. It's good none of them decided to try.

We welcome both crews of HMS Resolution to our shores as guests and to our waters for their tests.

Their missile was a bullseye and the manners and conduct of her crew have scored similar bulleyes among our people in Brevard.

We hope they never will have to fire their missiles in anger but are glad they are so finely tuned if the call comes.

A newspaper report of HMS *Resolution*'s first missile launch.

Left: CPE introduces the Resident Officer Polaris Executive (ROPE) to the First Sea Lord at Faslane in 1967. (Open Government Licence v3.0)

Below: The galley on HMS *Revenge*.

A Polaris missile second-stage test firing from Observation Island.

HMS *Revenge* leaving Faslane for the last time in 1992.

HMS *Resolution* decommissioning booklet.

2

BRITAIN AND THE BOMB

Towards the end of August 1945, the recently elected Labour Prime Minister, Clement Attlee, formed a committee that became known as Gen 75. Membership of Gen 75 initially consisted of five ministers: the Prime Minister, Clement Attlee; the Lord President of the Council, Herbert Morrison; the Foreign Secretary, Ernest Bevin; and the President of the Board of Trade, Stafford Cripps. A little later the membership was increased when the Lord Privy Seal, Arthur Greenwood, and the Chancellor of the Exchequer, Hugh Dalton were seconded. After the Gen 75 Committee decided that the nuclear weapons project should be the responsibility of the Ministry of Supply, the Minister of Supply, John Wilmot, was added. Attlee referred to this small group as the 'Bomb Committee', and it was to take the decisions that committed the country to the costly nuclear weapons programme; it also started Labour's troubled and uncomfortable relationship with nuclear weapons. Neither Parliament nor the Cabinet were involved, a secretive philosophy that was to persist throughout the country's nuclear weapons programme. Although the decision to actually 'build the bomb' was not taken until 1946, it seemed to be understood that the country should, or even needed to, produce its own nuclear weapons. Minutes from an early Gen 75 meeting showed that the committee members were more than aware of the importance of nuclear weapons and the associated research programmes, not only from a military point of view but also from the industrial perspective. They also felt it was important for the country's world standing and to secure American cooperation in future research. The committee was of the opinion that the country should take full advantage of a discovery in which Britain had a leading role in from the very beginning.

The military advantages were reiterated by the Chiefs of Staff, particularly the RAF who believed that Britain was very vulnerable to a nuclear attack and the only possible defence was for the country to have its own arsenal of nuclear weapons. Two years later, in 1947, they were of the opinion that even with American assistance, Britain could not prevent the vastly superior Russian forces from overrunning Western Europe, from where Russia could obliterate Britain with missiles without having to use nuclear weapons. The Chiefs of Staff reasoned that only by threatening to retaliate with nuclear weapons that would result in substantial damage could the Russians be prevented from using nuclear weapons in a war.

To supply the plutonium required for the programme, one of the committee's first decisions was to build several nuclear reactors and as a by-product created the British nuclear power electric generation industry. Air Marshall Viscount Portal of Hungerford, the former Chief of the Air Staff, was appointed as Controller of Production, Atomic Energy (CPAE). His small staff included some of the civil servants who had been involved in the Tube Alloys project (the British nuclear weapon programme that started during the war). Sir John Crockcroft, the British physicist, who was to share the Nobel Prize for Physics in 1951, was appointed Director of the Atomic Energy Research Establishment (AERE). Christopher Hinton (a senior ICI engineer) became the leader of the fissile material production programme. During 1946 the committee determined where the first sites for this programme should be situated. Two mainly civilian sites would be located at Harwell, Oxfordshire, for the AERE research centre, and Risley in Lancashire for Hinton's industrial centre. The country's first nuclear reactors were built at Harwell, named GLEEP, which started operations in August 1947 and at the time was the first nuclear reactor in Western Europe, and BEPO, which went critical on 3 July 1948.

Why the Government decided on such an expensive and potentially divisive course of action in setting up its own programme is open to debate; they came under constant pressure from Hugh Dalton and Sir Stafford Cripps to cancel the bomb project due to its cost. However, there was no guarantee that the Americans would continue to cooperate on the bomb project and the McMahon Act of 1946 restricted foreign access to American nuclear technology. This may have influenced the British decision 'to go it alone', although the overriding reason was undoubtedly national and perhaps not a small amount of personal pride, boosted by a smattering of individual ego. Britain still pictured itself as a major global player and some of the committee members undoubtedly wanted nuclear weapons to bolster Britain's standing on the world stage and claim its place, its rightful place, in the very exclusive nuclear weapons club. In October 1946, the Bomb Committee held a meeting where it was agreed that to build a gaseous diffusion plant, which would enrich the uranium required to build the nuclear bomb, was too expensive and should not be pursued. Ernest Bevin arrived late from attending a particularly unpleasant meeting with the American Secretary of State. He announced:

> We've got to have this thing. I don't mind it for myself, but I don't want any other Foreign Secretary of this country to be talked at or to by the Secretary of State of the US as I have just been … We've got to have this thing over here, whatever it costs … We've got to have the bloody Union Jack on top of it.

Politicians, particularly Bevin and Attlee, saw a British nuclear bomb as a relatively cheap way of ensuring the country's 'first league status'; not having it would lead to a loss of prestige, influence and international respect that would be more than the nation could endure.

There were other reasons, in truth probably as many reasons as there were committee members, and each member may well have had several reasons for supporting this particular course of action.

The members of the committee had lived through the two worst wars in history. If the effects of the nuclear bomb were so terrible that it would cause a potential enemy to pause and reconsider his action, then it was a price worth paying. Essentially this new weapon could end all wars and any Government's first responsibility is to protect its own people. This was a sentiment echoed by the scientist who developed the American bomb. After the first one was dropped on Hiroshima they asked if it was big enough. Not big enough to destroy the city but big enough to end the war, hopefully all wars.

On a more practical level, the bomb appeared to offer a cheaper option than conventional forces and this would allow these to be cut, saving money that could be better spent elsewhere. Also, as the Chiefs of Staff pointed out, in post-war Europe the nuclear bomb seemed the only realistic way of preventing Russian advances as no European country could afford to match the Soviet army man for man.

As highlighted in the minutes of the Gen 75 committee, they considered that there would be important industrial 'spin-offs', not least of which would be the production of cheap electrical power. This would be so cheap, if one believed the early adverts for the nuclear reactors, that it wouldn't be worth metering it. Although this dream was never realised, it did provide a popular justification for the fledgling nuclear weapons programme.

National standing and costs aside, it was with some justification that Britain felt it was entitled to be involved in the nuclear bomb project. Arguably the first real proof that the concept would work originated in Britain. Although nuclear research was being carried out in several countries, during September 1932, within seven months of the discovery of the neutron and more than six years before the splitting of the atom, the Austro–Hungarian Physicist Leo Szilard conceived the possibility of a neutron-induced chain reaction that would release large amounts of energy. In March 1934, while carrying out research at Oxford, he filed a patent on the 'application' of the neutron chain reaction. He was so worried about the possible consequences of this research that in an almost visionary moment of what was to come, he assigned the patent to the Admiralty. In 1938, he moved to America and along with fellow physicists Eugene Wigner and Edward Teller drafted a letter to the American President, stating that it was probable that a chain reaction, using uranium, would release large amounts of energy, and if this chain reaction was not controlled a massive explosion would result. The physicists predicted it would be possible to build very powerful bombs using this principle, and they expressed their concerns that the Germans would be first to develop the bomb. This letter was signed by Albert Einstein and prompted President Roosevelt to start a project to investigate these claims, initially as part of the National Bureau of Standards. It was not given a particularly high priority and the project got off to a slow start.

Churchill had already decided to intiate the bomb project, and to that end the Directorate of 'Tube Alloys' was formed within the Department of Scientific and Industrial Research, under the technical leadership of W.A. Akers, a physicist recruited from Imperial Chemical Industries. Sir John Anderson, Lord President of the Council, provided policy guidance.

During February 1940, Otto Frisch and Rudolf Peierls, working in Britain, developed the first critical mass calculation for uranium 235, and this was detailed in the Frisch–Peierls memorandum. As a result of this, the Uranium Subcommittee was formed, which reported to the Committee for the Scientific Survey of Air Warfare. This in turn led to the formation of the MAUD Committee (supposedly named after the nanny of one of the committee members, or perhaps it stood for Military Application of Uranium Detonation), whose purpose was to evaluate and comment on Frisch's and Peierl's findings. It was chaired by Sir Henry Tizard and between 10 April 1940 and 15 July 1941 produced the basic principles of both the fission bomb design and uranium enrichment by gaseous diffusion. This work was instrumental in alerting America (and unfortunately by espionage, Russia) to the possibility of constructing viable nuclear weapons.

Two reports were produced and sent to the British Government regarding the employment of uranium as a source of power and its use in a bomb. The latter drew three conclusions:

1. The Frisch–Peierls scheme for producing a uranium bomb was feasible.
2. Work towards building such a bomb should receive the highest priority.
3. Close cooperation with America was of the utmost importance.

At this stage of the war Britain desperately needed American assistance in any shape or form. France had fallen and the country was being subjected to nightly bombing raids. Radar would greatly help Britain deal with these raids and British scientists had made a technical breakthrough with the cavity magnetron (a high-powdered vacuum tube that produces microwaves). However, Britain had neither the money nor the factory capacity needed to produce these in anything like the numbers needed. Henry Tizard, who was also chairman of the Aeronautical Research Committee, suggested to Churchill that a 'technological exchange' would solve this problem; the cavity magnetron would be gifted to the Americans in return for them mass producing the device. Churchill was very uncomfortable about giving away such innovative and potentially valuable technology. Tizard intended to 'share' not only the magnetron but the gyroscopic gun sights, Frank Whittle's jet engine and the initial findings of the MAUD Committee. Unfortunately the country was in such a perilous position that Churchill had little choice but to agree. In late September 1940, representatives from the British military and scientific communities travelled to America. Tizard led the delegation and it became known as the Tizard Mission, or the British Technical and Scientific Mission. Apart from the technological exchange, they also explored the possibility of relocating the British military research facilities to North America, where they could work undisturbed by German bombers, or avoid falling into German hands if the country was invaded.

Initially the MAUD Committee report was not circulated in the US, delaying any response. When it was eventually seen by the appropriate people, the Americans changed their minds about the feasibility of producing an atomic bomb and suggested that America and Britain should cooperate on the project. Harold C. Urey, the Nobel physical chemist, and George Braxton Pegram were sent to Britain in November 1941 to make the necessary arrangements but at this stage Britain did not take up the offer of collaboration. Despite the British reluctance to become involved, the exchange of information continued until the middle of 1942. At this stage the British had doubts about whether or not the project could be brought to a successful conclusion. At this time Sir John Anderson proposed further cooperation between the two countries but the American project had been transferred to the army under the command of General L.R. Groves. He was of the opinion that the British could make no further useful contribution to the project and this resulted in further restrictions on the information exchange between the two countries.

In July 1943 Dr Vannevar Bush, who was Director of the Office of Scientific Research and Development, and Henry Stimson, the American Secretary of War, visited London and met with Churchill. Many of the problems and misunderstandings regarding nuclear weapon research were addressed and resolved. It was decided that Britain should draft an agreement that would define the terms for future collaboration; this became known as the Quebec Arrangement. It was signed by Churchill and Roosevelt on 19 August 1943. The agreement committed both countries to:

Never use this agency against each other.
Not use it against third parties without each other's consent.
Not communicate any information about Tube Alloys to third parties except by mutual consent.

It was also agreed that any post-war advantages of an industrial or commercial nature would be decided at the discretion of the American President.

Once the two countries restarted exchanging information, the British realised how far behind the Americans were, and the senior British advisor to the Combined Policy Committee, Professor James Chadwick, advised that it would be wiser if they stopped their research programme in Britain and put all available resources into assisting the Americans. As a result of this, approximately forty British scientists, 'the British Mission', were sent to work at Los Alamos on 19 August 1943. They were fully integrated into the American teams and eventually several became team leaders. Among them were Geoffrey I. Taylor, the pioneer of shock wave physics, and William G. Penney, who, after the war was to lead the British nuclear bomb programme. The British team made major contributions to the Manhattan Project and provided the nucleus for the country's post-war nuclear weapons programme. Unfortunately one of the British team was Klaus Fuchs, a German communist, who provided detailed information to the Russians and undoubtedly coloured American attitudes to Britain over the next few years. The Russians were given details of British initial research by Fuchs and possibly John Cairncross. A report by Lavrentiy Beria, chief of Soviet security and the NKVD secret police, to Stalin in March 1942 had the MAUD report and other British documents attached.

At the end of the war the British Government believed that the Americans would continue to share the technology, which the British saw as a joint discovery. However, the passing of the McMahon Act (Atomic Energy Act) by the Truman administration in August 1946 made it clear that Britain would no longer be allowed access to American atomic research. This was in part due to the arrest of Alan Nunn May, a British physicist working on the Manhattan Project in Canada, who passed atomic secrets to the Russians. He was arrested for espionage in 1946. The act seemed to be a direct contradiction of the 'Hyde Park Agreement', where the President and Prime Minister agreed that the wartime collaboration would continue until Japan was defeated or the agreement was terminated by mutual understanding. The Americans seemed to have misfiled this document and it was not found until the mid 1950s.

Filing errors aside, the experience and knowledge gained by the British scientific team during the Manhattan Project was invaluable to its nuclear weapons programme, particularly after the Americans imposed another information ban in the 1950s. The British nuclear bomb project progressed satisfactorily and on 3 October 1952 Britain's first nuclear weapon, Hurricane, was detonated in a lagoon off the western shore of Trimouille Island. Britain acquired its first deployed weapon, the Blue Danube plutonium bomb, in November 1953. Plans at this point called for building up an arsenal of 200 weapons by 1957 so plutonium production was expanded by adding two new dual-use (plutonium and electricity) Magnox reactors at Calder Hall. These nuclear weapons would be free fall bombs that would be dropped by the RAF's V bomber force. Until Britain had a sufficient number of nuclear weapons, America supplied them under a programme that became known as Project E, an arrangement that started in 1958. However, with improvements in Russian air defence systems it soon became apparent that a ballistic missile was the only way the country could maintain a credible deterrent. Politicians felt that an independent deterrent was the only way of ensuring that Britain would remain a major world power. It was thought that the use of an American missile would have handed control of the British deterrent to the Americans, a dilemma that was to haunt British politicians over the coming years.

America exploded the first hydrogen bomb (super bomb) on 1 November 1952, at Enewetak in the Marshall Islands. After the dropping of atomic bombs on Japan, the Americans had not pursued the development of the hydrogen bomb until the Russians successfully detonated an atomic bomb in 1949. Nearly a year later, on 12 August 1953, Russia detonated a hydrogen bomb at the Semipalatinsk test site in northern Kazakhstan. Unlike the first Russian atomic bomb, the development of which was fast-tracked by the aid of British spies and espionage in America, this bomb was of an original Russian design.

After the detonation of the American and Russian thermonuclear weapons, Britain deployed an 'interim megaton weapon' carried on the RAF's V-bomber aircraft, until a true thermonuclear weapon could be produced. The decision to develop this more powerful weapon was generally accepted in the House of Commons and surprisingly even the press were supportive, including many of the papers that were normally critical of the Government. The *Manchester Guardian* thought the decision sound, and believed that the Government was right to develop a powerful deterrent, especially in the absence of a close partnership with the Americans. However, the paper did criticise the government for using bombers rather than missiles to deliver the

Above: Admiralty Floating Dock (AFD) 60 in the early 1990s. (Open Government License v3.0)

Left: The waterfront in the early 1980s. (Open Government License v3.0)

HMS *Repulse*. (Open Government License v3.0)

An unusual picture of three quarters of the flotilla. This photograph was taken when HMS *Renown* came out of her long refit period. The lead submarine is HMS *Resolution*. (Open Government License v3.0)

HMS *Revenge*. (Open Government License v3.0)

HMS *Repulse*. (Open Government License v3.0)

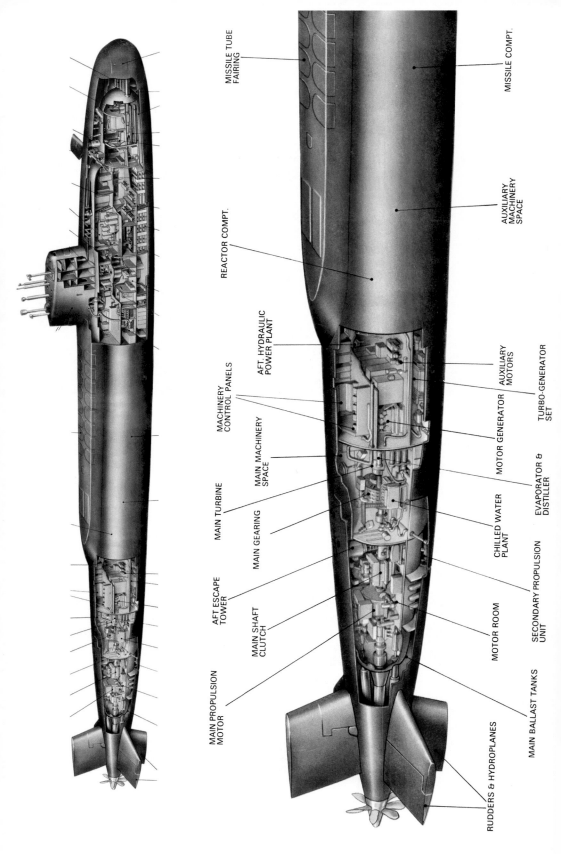

MISSILE TUBE FAIRING

MISSILE COMPT.

REACTOR COMPT.

AUXILIARY MACHINERY SPACE

AFT. HYDRAULIC POWER PLANT

MACHINERY CONTROL PANELS

AUXILIARY MOTORS

MOTOR GENERATOR

TURBO-GENERATOR SET

MAIN MACHINERY SPACE

MAIN TURBINE

MAIN GEARING

EVAPORATOR & DISTILLER

CHILLED WATER PLANT

AFT ESCAPE TOWER

MAIN SHAFT CLUTCH

SECONDARY PROPULSION UNIT

MOTOR ROOM

MAIN PROPULSION MOTOR

MAIN BALLAST TANKS

RUDDERS & HYDROPLANES

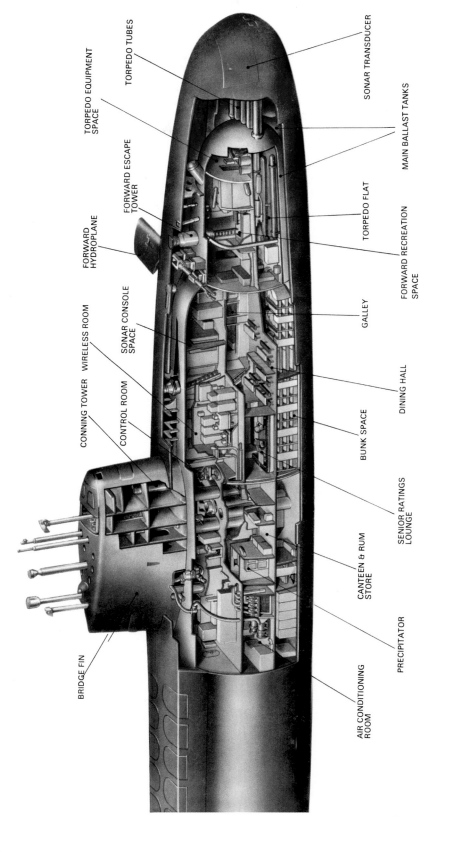

TORPEDO EQUIPMENT SPACE

TORPEDO TUBES

SONAR TRANSDUCER

MAIN BALLAST TANKS

FORWARD ESCAPE TOWER

TORPEDO FLAT

FORWARD HYDROPLANE

FORWARD RECREATION SPACE

GALLEY

WIRELESS ROOM

SONAR CONSOLE SPACE

CONNING TOWER

CONTROL ROOM

DINING HALL

BUNK SPACE

SENIOR RATINGS LOUNGE

CANTEEN & RUM STORE

PRECIPITATOR

BRIDGE FIN

AIR CONDITIONING ROOM

Senior rates mess.

Wardroom.

Junior rates recreation space.

(Open Government License v3.0)

The rededication of the Polaris Stone.

Polaris Monument
This monument was rededicated on
23rd April 2013 in recognition of the
50th anniversary
of the signing of the Polaris Sales Agreement.
Rear Admiral M A Beverstock, CSSE
Rear Admiral T J Benedict USN, DIRSSP
'Pacem per Vires'

weapons. Even the 'left-leaning' press, including *The Economist* and *The New Statesman*, supported the policy, although this was primarily on the grounds that it would be a means of reducing the expenditure on the country's conventional forces.

In April 1954 the Americans proposed a joint development programme; they would develop an intercontinental ballistic missile (ICBM) of 5,000 nautical mile (9,300 km) range while Britain, with support from the Americans, would develop a medium-range ballistic missile (MRBM) with 2,000 nautical mile range. This suited Britain, as the RAF's V bombers were due to be retired in 1965, and the proposal was agreed as part of the Wilson–Sandys Agreement in August 1954. This provided for collaboration, exchange of information, and mutual planning in the development of weapon programmes. The Government also hoped that the agreement would provide an opportunity to learn more about missile design and development from the Americans.

De Havilland won the contract to build the missile and the proposed rocket became known as Blue Streak. Almost immediately doubts arose over the cost as they escalated from the initial estimate of £50 million submitted to the Treasury in early 1955, to £300 million by late 1959. There were also complaints about progress of the programme compared with the speed of development in America and Russia. The project was eventually cancelled in 1960 and while mounting costs undoubtedly played a part in the decision, it was its lack of credibility as an effective deterrent that sealed its fate. The missiles were fuelled by liquid oxygen and kerosene. The kerosene could be 'left' in the missile, but liquid oxygen had to be loaded immediately before launch. This process took approximately fifteen minutes and during this period the missiles were susceptible to a pre-emptive attack, essentially abolishing any deterrent effect. To overcome this, it was suggested that the missiles could be stowed in underground silos, which could be designed to withstand a 1 megaton blast at a distance of half a mile (another British innovation, subsequently exported to America). Finding sites for the silos proved difficult, primarily due to the country's small size, and in the end only one was constructed at RAF Spadeadam in Cumbria. Understandably there was a reluctance to cancel the project, primarily because of the huge costs incurred. It was suggested that Blue Streak would become the first stage of a proposed all British satellite launcher that would become known as Black Prince; the second stage was derived from the Blue Streak test vehicle Black Knight. This project never progressed beyond the design stage, although Blue Streak was used as the first stage of the European Launcher Development Organisation (ELDO) in conjunction with the French and Germans. The Blue Streak first stage was successfully tested three times at the Woomera test range in Australia as part of the ELDO programme.

Later in the year, on 5 November 1954, the Ministry of Supply issued a memorandum suggesting that by 1960 the Russian air defences would be sufficiently advanced to make an attack by the RAF's V bombers, carrying the current free-fall nuclear bombs, unlikely to be successful. It proposed a nuclear-armed missile that had a range of approximately 50 miles and could be carried by the V force, would keep the bombers out of range of Russian ground-to-air area defence missiles. The Ministry of Supply chose the British aircraft manufacture Avro, which had manufactured the Lancaster and later the Vulcan, to produce this weapon. The missile was Blue Steel; an air-launched, rocket-propelled nuclear stand-off missile. Entering service in February 1963, it was the primary British nuclear deterrent weapon until it was officially retired on 31 December 1970, when strategic nuclear deterrent passed to the Royal Navy's Polaris submarine fleet.

Avro proposed that subsequent versions of the missile would have increased speed (up to Mach 4.5) and range. Eventually it would have a range of 900 nautical miles and be capable of being launched by the supersonic Avro 730, which was under development. Similar to Blue Streak, the missile was fuelled by a combination of hydrogen peroxide and kerosene. Fuelling the missile before take-off took nearly half an hour and the nature of the fuel made it quite a hazardous operation.

Until August 1957 Europe could safely sit under the American nuclear umbrella. Things got a little more challenging when the Russians successfully launched the world's first intercontinental ballistic missile (ICBM) and two months later, on 4 October 1957, launched the first Earth-orbiting satellite, Sputnik. This proved beyond doubt that the Russians had a launch vehicle capable of striking America with a nuclear weapon. It also started the space race that culminated in the Apollo Moon landings, with astronaut Frank Borman viewing these as just a battle in the Cold War. The powerful rockets required to carry out these impressive spaceflights indicated improved, more advanced ICBMs. Some in the West thought that America would abandon its Western allies, not wishing to risk a nuclear strike on its home territory for the sake of Europe. This may have further influenced Britain's intentions to have a totally independent deterrent.

Harold Macmillan became Prime Minister on 10 January 1957 in the wake of Antony Eden's sudden resignation. He summed up the central theme of his administration, and of the progressive Conservatism he represented, as interdependence. By this he meant that Britain should be at the centre of an interdependent Commonwealth and an interdependent Western Europe while retaining all the rights of a sovereign state, especially in nuclear defence. In October 1957, after a series of meetings in Washington with President Eisenhower, they issued a joint Declaration of Common Purpose, in which they affirmed they would collaborate in combating communism. They also reiterated their commitment to Anglo–American unity. In private, the two leaders agreed that their governments would work closely together in defence matters, particularly concerning nuclear weapons. Macmillan also saw these meetings as a welcome relaxing of America's attitude in the aftermath of the Suez Crisis and a return to the friendlier relationship enjoyed previously.

The nuclear collaboration between the two countries was formalised in the 1958 Agreement for Co-operation on the use of Atomic Energy for Mutual Defence Purposes. The agreement allowed for the exchange of classified information concerning the design, development and fabrication of nuclear weapons. It also allowed Britain to use the Nevada test site, work with American colleagues at Lawrence Livermore, Los Alamos, and Sandia National Laboratories, and also provided for extensive American assistance with all aspects of the British nuclear weapons programme.

Also in 1958, America and Russia temporarily suspended nuclear testing, although this informal agreement ended in September 1961 when Russia resumed it. America responded by conducting its own series of nuclear tests, and these resulted in both radioactive and political fallout. The public concern about the fallout danger finally produced enough political pressure to force negotiations towards a formal agreement; the Limited Test Ban Treaty (LTBT). This was a trilateral deal between America, Russia and Britain that stopped atmospheric, underwater and outer space nuclear tests. Since 1963, an additional 113 countries have signed the treaty. Two countries did not sign, France and China, although thirty-three years later they both signed the Comprehensive Test Ban Treaty (1996).

As part of the nuclear sharing strategy the Americans had intended to deploy Thor missiles in Britain for some time and during January 1957 British

Defence Minister Duncan Sandys proposed that the country should adopt this policy. He was a firm believer in the importance of missiles and was deeply involved in the Blue Streak programme. His support for this proposal was further influenced by the fact that Blue Streak would not be ready for deployment for a number of years, so the prospect of an interim IRBM deterrent was a very attractive option. It would cost Britain nothing except for the site preparation and to avoid political complications the weapons would be manned by the Royal Air Force, although the nuclear warheads would remain under American control. Macmillan saw it as an indication that Anglo–American relationships were being re-established after the Suez Crisis. He also saw it as a way of acquiring American missile technology and furthering his policy of interdependence. Although this term was used by both sides it had different meanings to each; America saw it as a method of centralising control, whereas Macmillan viewed it as a true partnership of equals.

In early 1958 the British Chief of the Air Staff was of the opinion that the proposed Thor deployment was designed to suit American aims more than British ones. He went on to point out that the missiles would never fully be under British control; it would make Britain a target and, similar to Blue Streak, the missiles were vulnerable to first strike. Final agreement on the deployment was reached at the Bermuda Conference of March 1957, when Macmillan and Eisenhower met to discuss various key issues. On 1 April Macmillan reassured Parliament that the missiles would be owned by the British Government and they would be manned by British troops, who would be trained by American experts. The missiles could only be launched by British personnel, but the warheads would remain under the control of the Americans, in accordance with US law. Macmillan stressed that this arrangement would not affect Britain's control of the targeting and launching of the missiles.

There was considerable opposition to the deployment, particularly from members of the general public who were gradually becoming organised in their expression of disapproval of nuclear weapons. Despite this, the Thor deployment went ahead and in February 1958 a joint government agreement was signed. The American Third Air Force would assist in the construction of the Thor sites and deliver the missiles, while the RAF would maintain and control them. Targeting would be a matter of joint operational policy between the US Strategic Air Command and RAF Bomber Command. Sixty Thor missiles were to be supplied to Britain;

these would be operated by twenty re-formed Royal Air Force squadrons with three missiles each.

By the late 1950s it was more than apparent that the Blue Streak programme was in trouble and when Macmillan met Eisenhower at Camp David during March 1959 he broached the possibility of Britain buying the Skybolt missile, then under development in America, which would be deployed by the V bomber force. The possibility of basing American Polaris submarines in Britain was also raised by the American President. Both these were ratified a year later, again at a meeting at Camp David, on 29 March 1960. Britain agreed to purchase 144 Skybolt missiles; funding for research and development was limited to that required to modify the V bombers to take the missile, but the British were allowed to fit their own warheads. At the same meeting, it was agreed that the Americans should be given nuclear submarine basing facilities in Scotland. Following the agreement, the Blue Streak programme was formally cancelled in April 1960 and a month later an agreement for an initial order of 100 Skybolts was placed. Although it has been suggested that the Americans agreed to sell Skybolt in exchange for Britain allowing them to base submarines in the Holy Loch, the two leaders never specifically mentioned this and only one document from the meetings mentioned the link. Between 1961 and 1992, Holy Loch was the site of the United States Navy's FBM Refit Site One (FBM: Fleet Ballistic Missile). It was the home base of Submarine Squadron (SUBRON) 14, part of Submarine Force, US Atlantic Fleet. To make maximum usage of its submarine-launched ballistic missile (SLBM) deterrent force, the American military had determined that it required an overseas base for refit and crew turnover. Interestingly, at a Cabinet meeting held on 20 June 1960, the British Minister of Defence, Harold Watkinson, said that during a meeting with his American opposite number he had explained that it would be easier to justify the basing of American submarines in Britain to the general public if it were presented as a joint project and the Americans gave Britain the option to buy or build Polaris submarines. It was also agreed that Loch Linnhe should be offered as the base if it had the required facilities for the Americans.

Skybolt was a very attractive option for the British Government; the launch platform already existed and its greater range, 1,150 miles against Blue Steel's 150, would allow the V bombers to launch their missiles while flying over the North Sea, well out of the range of any Russian ABM. Regardless of the apparent advantages of Skybolt, in April 1960 the Liberal

Party under Jo Grimond saw fit to call 'for the abandonment, not only of Blue Streak but the whole independent British deterrent':

> Is the Minister seriously saying to the people of this country that the Government are going on with this policy, which has proved such a disastrous waste and failure? Are they going to encourage the American Government to go on with Skybolt, or to spend an astronomical sum of money on some alternative? Does not this mark the absolute failure of the policy of the independent deterrent? Is it not the case that everybody else in the world knew this, except the Conservative Party in this country? Is it not the case that the Americans gave up production of the B52, which was to carry Skybolt, nine months ago? Does the Minister of Defence read the evidence given before the Congressional Committee, which has been critical of Skybolt for 2½ years? Will he give an assurance to the House that we shall not embark on Polaris without a reasonable estimate of what it will cost, and a more reliable estimate of the chance of success being put before the people of this country?

When John Kennedy became American President later in 1960 he tasked his Secretary of Defence, Robert McNamara, to formulate a new nuclear defence policy that did not rely on the Eisenhower-era obsession with nuclear retaliation. He started with a series of initiatives and an entirely new defence philosophy. While he believed that America should maintain her nuclear supremacy, he proposed a policy of 'flexible response' as opposed to the 'massive retaliation' favoured by the previous administration. When he first became President he quoted to Congress from General Maxwell Taylor's book *The Uncertainty Trumpet*. In its conclusion it stated that the policy of massive retaliation essentially left the country with only two choices: surrender or face total obliteration.

The new administration also had a very different view of the special relationship; generally it was opposed to the British independent deterrent, McNamara being particularly against the idea. He made a speech on 16 June 1962 at Ann Arbor, Michigan, where he pointed out that countries with limited nuclear capabilities that operated independently were dangerous, expensive, and prone to obsolescence, and their deterrent value was limited at best.

Meanwhile, Dean Acheson, the former Secretary of State, in a speech at West Point, insensitively pointed out that while Britain had lost an empire it was struggling to find a new role and that any role based on the much-valued special relationship with America was about played out.

The Kennedy administration also had a much more business-like attitude towards Skybolt and saw the ever-increasing costs and persisting technical difficulties as major obstacles. At one stage an American official informed British Chief Scientific Officer Solly Zuckerman that the technical problems that needed to be resolved before Skybolt could become operational were formidable. Macmillan was very concerned, his whole Government's nuclear deterrence policy was based on Skybolt and if the programme was cancelled or postponed so soon after obtaining Parliament's agreement it would be disastrous, and the Government would in all probability fall. The Minister of Defence, Harold Watkinson, attempted to downplay the significance of Skybolt by claiming that it was not an essential part of British defence policy. He pointed out that the development of the Blue Steel missile and the TSR-2 aircraft would adequately meet the country's nuclear deterrent requirements. Not surprisingly, Lord Mountbatten (the Chief of Defence Staff) suggested that, in the event of Skybolt being cancelled, the money set aside for Skybolt should be used to buy Polaris, and he insisted that the Americans should be obliged to offer Britain another form of deterrent if they chose to cancel Skybolt.

The cancellation was finally announced in a minute from the American embassy in London on 11 December 1962. McNamara flew to Britain to explain the decision to Thornycroft and was bluntly informed that this was totally unacceptable to the British Government. The British press blasted the Kennedy administration for its tactlessness and infidelity, and in Parliament there was talk of reprisals and 'an agonising reappraisal' of the special relationship. This became known as the Skybolt crisis.

Two days later Macmillan sent a message to the British Ambassador in Washington suggesting that the Skybolt question should be at the top of the agenda at the forthcoming Nassau meeting. His rationale was that if they could not reach a suitable agreement that would ensure the continuation of the British independent deterrent, a radical and probably very painful review of all foreign and defence policy would be required.

On 21 December 1962, President Kennedy and Prime Minister Harold Macmillan announced the formation of a multilateral NATO nuclear force after talks in Nassau, in the Bahamas. The agreement paved the way for America to sell Polaris missiles to Britain.

The President also sent a letter to President de Gaulle offering to sell Polaris as well as provide technical support, in the hope of establishing a tripartite nuclear deterrent against the Eastern Bloc. He also hoped this would settle the differences between France and Britain over Macmillan's special relationship with America and assist Britain's aspirations to join the European Economic Community (EEC); Kennedy believed it would strengthen NATO and allow France a greater role within it.

At the end of the three-day meeting the two leaders issued a joint statement. Macmillan made it clear that Polaris missiles would be used in the defence of NATO countries, except where Britain's supreme national interests were at stake, a phrase he hoped would show the British nuclear force was, at least politically, independent of American influence.

On his return, the Prime Minister happily assured the country that it now had a weapon that would last a generation and that the terms were very good. He had done very well to persuade the Americans to give him Polaris and on the terms he wanted, as the favoured American option was for Britain to keep funding Skybolt or take the Hound Dog missile.

In spite of this, many expressed concerns that Britain would be too reliant on America for its nuclear deterrent, regardless of the fact that the warheads would be supplied by Britain. At the time it was reported in one American newspaper that the first of a dozen Polaris submarines would be due to go into service in the UK within five years.

Macmillan later wrote about the meeting that the President did not want to give Britain Polaris primarily on political grounds; he did not want to upset those European nations that had no nuclear weapon development programme. Meanwhile, Macmillan felt that Britain had a right to Polaris and was determined to acquire the missile for Britain. He assured the President that, once the system was operational, it would be made available to NATO.

However, not everybody shared Macmillan's enthusiasm for the new missile system. Many worried about the costs; although the Government would not pay any of the $800 million development cost of the system, it had paid $28 million into Skybolt and it had now committed itself to spending $1 billion more for the submarines and the associated support facilities. Some felt that it would leave the country over-dependent on America. There was also concern over the fact that there could be a gap of several years between the date when Britain's bomber force would become obsolete and the commissioning of the first submarine. Even members of the Prime Minister's own party were sceptical of the fact that the submarines would be part of a multi-lateral NATO force except in circumstances of supreme national interest. Who would decide what justified national interest, and what would happen if those national interests conflicted with American policy were left unaddressed.

On 10 April 1963 Macmillan and Kennedy signed the Nassau Agreement that allowed Britain to purchase the A3 missile system and thereby saved the credibility of the Macmillan Government, providing the Royal Navy could deliver.

France eventually rejected America's offer and the multilateral NATO nuclear agreement was signed without the country in January 1963. In his desire for independence from the superpowers and wanting to play a major role on the world stage, de Gaulle ensured that France developed its own nuclear arsenal. It also withdrew its military bodies from NATO command in 1966 but remained in the alliance's political councils. Whether or not France's inclusion in the offer was a deliberate ploy by Kennedy to end Britain's cherished special relationship with America is open to debate. France refused the offer and was quick to point out that Britain's ties with America had caused nothing but humiliation, providing further justification for France's decision to develop its own nuclear weapon systems. De Gaulle had argued that the Atlantic alliance should be run by France, America and Britain, each an equal partner. This was one of his major, if unspoken, conditions for British membership of the Common Market and he suggested to Macmillan that it would help if Britain were to share its advanced missile technology with France. When Macmillan replied noncommittally that he would have to discuss this with Kennedy, de Gaulle told his guest that France in that case could do nothing to ease Britain's entry into Europe. Unfortunately the Nassau agreement only further confirmed de Gaulle's conviction that Britain was a 'Trojan horse' that would allow America a voice in Europe. This was the main reason he vetoed Britain's application for membership of the EEC in 1963 and then again in 1967.

The Americans also planned to supply the Italian Navy with the Polaris missile, although this agreement ended in the mid 1960s despite several successful test launches being carried out on board the Italian cruiser *Giuseppe Garibaldi*. The Americans never provided the missiles and the Italians developed an indigenous missile, called Alfa. This was ended by the Nuclear Non-Proliferation Treaty ratification and the failure of the NATO Multilateral Force.

As early as 1955 Churchill had stated that deterrence would be the route to disarmament and unless Britain contributed to Western deterrence with its own weapons, targets that might threaten Britain might not be targeted by NATO. It was a view echoed a little later by Harold Macmillan when he pronounced that nuclear weapons would give Britain influence over targeting and American policy, and would affect strategy in the Middle East and Far East.

Despite this, British politicians, as a class, seemed to have had difficulty in understanding the concept of deterrence, or accepting the morality of nuclear weapons, particularly members of the left wing of the Labour Party. That said, they generally supported British nuclear weapons programmes but opposed tests. Labour leader Hugh Gaitskell and shadow Foreign Secretary Aneurin Bevan agreed with Duncan Sandys on the importance of reducing dependence on the American deterrent. Even the left-wing Bevan told his colleagues that their demand for unilateral nuclear disarmament would send a future Labour government naked into the conference chamber during international negotiations. The Labour Party was also put under a lot of pressure by the trade unions who, despite many of their members being dependent on the nuclear programme for a living, were generally not in favour of the nuclear weapon programme. In fact, some trade unions were affiliated to the Campaign for Nuclear Disarmament (CND) and during the 1950s and '60s nuclear weapons were often denounced at the TUC's annual conference.

In the early 1960s, NATO began to examine proposals for a new nuclear-armed naval force; one of these was the Multilateral [Nuclear] Force (MLF). It would consist of approximately twenty-five destroyers, each armed with six Polaris missiles. These vessels would be under the command of the Strategic Allied Commander Europe (SACEUR) in NATO and patrol friendly waters of the North Atlantic and Mediterranean area. Controversially, it was proposed that these ships should be built, owned and manned jointly by the various participant countries. The mixed manning proposal was particularly unpopular with military chiefs from all countries. However, it was the top slot American foreign policy during 1963 and 1964, and despite numerous objections it certainly seemed the proposal would become reality. These proposals were warmly welcomed by Germany, but Britain had very strong reservations, doubting whether there was military justification for any substantial addition to the Alliance's strategic nuclear forces. Furthermore, the MLF would have involved considerable additional expenditure for all participants and a force without Britain would be dominated by America and Germany. Interestingly, during 1964 and 1965 an American destroyer carried out a joint manning exercise and this proved highly successful. Despite this, by the end of 1965 the MLF plan was, much to the relief of the military chiefs, dropped.

Just after the general election in October 1964, the newly elected Labour Prime Minister Harold Wilson suggested to his Foreign Secretary, Patrick Gordon Walker, that Britain should consider committing the fledgling Polaris submarine fleet to NATO. This proposal was to be called the Atlantic Nuclear Force (ANF) and was the major foreign policy initiative of the new Government. The idea was tentatively outlined in Washington to Dean Rusk in December 1964 and Walker proposed that its use should be agreed through a body where all participating European countries would be equal.

In December Britain formally proposed the ANF to its allies, essentially as an alternative to the MLF. The main difference between the two was that the Polaris submarines would not be mixed manned. America was reluctant to agree to or even consider this proposal as it included US Polaris submarines and Strategic Air Command aircraft. Another aspect of the December 1964 proposal was that if Britain were to effectively relinquish the 'supreme national interests' exemption clause in the Nassau Communiqué, it would not be easy to refuse a request to install Permissive Action Links (PALs) in British Polaris missiles. PALs were security devices that were intended to stop the unauthorised arming, launch or detonation of a nuclear weapon. With a multinational force it might be difficult to define who would 'authorise' the launch, particularly if Britain wished to use the weapons in a case of 'supreme national interests', and that is providing that the various countries could agree on what constituted such an incident.

In 1964 Labour committed to renegotiation the Polaris programme, primarily to appease the party's left wing. Wilson's intention was that the Polaris fleet would operate within the ANF as detailed above. Despite reassuring the public and his party that the whole Polaris requirement would be reassessed, Wilson told new US President Lyndon Johnson that Britain would remain a nuclear power.

Twenty years later, Labour leader Michael Foot wanted to commit the country to unilateral disarmament in his 1983 General Election manifesto, which became known as the longest suicide note in history. It said: 'We must use unilateral steps taken by Britain to secure multilateral solutions on the international level.' Campaigners for nuclear disarmament believed that if the country got rid of its nuclear weapons, others would follow suit. They argued this was a basis on which world peace and cooperation could be built, but unrest about the Cold War ensured that there was strong public opposition.

Foot's successor, Neil Kinnock, who became leader on 2 October 1983 after Foot resigned following the 1983 election defeat, single-handedly managed to make the deterrent all but redundant with his response to a question in a TV interview about whether or not he would press the button: 'I would die for my country but I could never allow my country to die for me.'

Labour's difficult relationship with nuclear weapons seems destined to continue; as I write, the future of the country's nuclear deterrent is causing problems for the new Labour leader at the annual party conference and, similar to Kinnock, he has publicly stated that if he was Prime Minister he would not give the command to launch Trident, essentially rendering the deterrent pointless.

Most other former prime ministers have supported the independent nuclear deterrent. Labour's James Callaghan believed he would not be able to forgive himself if he had to order a nuclear strike, although if the situation required it, he would press the button. Denis Healey, who was Secretary of State for Defence in Harold Wilson's Government, said that if the country was under nuclear attack and the Prime Minister had been killed, he would have ordered a nuclear counter-attack. In TV interviews ex-prime ministers Gordon Brown, Tony Blair and John Major all stated that in no circumstances would they order nuclear weapons to be launched against civilian targets – the basis being that a counter-attack would be a futile act of vengeance that would result in unacceptable levels of harm on a civilian population.

3

THE POLARIS PROJECT

It was while serving with the Plans Division within the Ministry of Defence in December 1962 that Captain J. Moore was asked to prepare a brief, out-lining the effects that the Polaris programme might have on the rest of the Royal Navy should it be introduced. The brief was required by the First Lord, who was going to brief the Cabinet the following day so they could advise the Prime Minister, who was in Nassau attending a meeting with President Kennedy. He had approximately eighteen hours to complete the task. With help from a variety of sources, including the previously completed prudent staff work, and by calling in a lifetime's worth of favours, he successfully fin-ished the work within the required time frame. Once briefed, the Cabinet duly advised the Prime Minister that the procurement of the Polaris system and its associate support network was a viable option for the nation. Captain Moore's paper was arguably one of the most important documents concerned with the Polaris project. The Macmillan Government was in a dilemma; Skybolt was probably going to be cancelled, leaving their nuclear strategy, at best, in a state of disarray. Their very credibility was at stake. If Macmillan came back with Polaris and it couldn't be made to work, he, his Government, and the country as a whole, would be a laughing stock, and the Conservative Government would surely fall. If Britain bought into Polaris it had to work, there was no other alternative. Captain Moore's paper was that confirmation.

It has long been the accepted view that before the arrival of Polaris the Royal Navy had no particular interest in the country's nuclear deterrent and had done little more than prudent staff work, concerning itself with its more traditional blue water fleet role. The Navy had understandable concerns about the financial costs that would be incurred if it took on the deterrent role, and the expected demands on skilled manpower only heightened reservations. While the Navy undoubtedly wanted to retain its traditional role, it certainly did not sit on its hands when it came to the replacement of the RAF's nuclear V bomber squadrons. The Navy had, in fact, run a comprehensive and shrewd campaign to assume the nuclear deterrent role and in this endeavour, for a variety of reasons, had received an extraordinary amount of support from the US Navy. This whole period shows that a little more-than-prudent staff work took place. That said, it would be wrong to view the Royal Navy as a single-minded entity; it might be best depicted as 'many minds, one heart'. There were many different and very vocal lobbies, all promoting or defending their own particular domain, be that aircraft carriers, the surface fleet, or submarines, both nuclear and conventional. It would be fair to say that support for the proposed Polaris programme was far from universal and there were certainly those in the Navy who viewed the Polaris lobby with a certain amount of unease. Even Mountbatten seemed to think that a national deterrent would not be feasible and that it should be incorporated into a European deterrent. This put him very much in line with the American view on how the British deterrent should be controlled.

Naval interest in nuclear power had been roused well before this and Captain Moore's paper could be considered the final act in a long campaign. In the aftermath of the Second World War, the three armed services carried out several reviews and studies on the possible applications of atomic power. The general conclusion was that perhaps in the future the armed services' primary aim would be 'the prevention of war rather than the ability to fight it'. Other conclusions reached were that the Director of Naval Air Warfare and Training (DAWT) suggested that the Navy could deliver atomic weapons against an enemy well beyond the range of missiles launched from Britain, while the Director of Naval Operational Research (DNOR) prophetically thought it might be possible to launch nuclear-armed rockets from submarines. It was the promise of high speeds and unlimited endurance that first kindled Flag Officer Submarines (FOSM) interest in nuclear power.

To this end, in 1946, the Admiralty appointed several naval officers and a member of the Royal Naval Scientific Service to the Atomic Energy Research Establishment at Harwell. A little later, during 1950, the Defence Research Policy Committee (DRPC), along with the heavy electrical manufacturing company Metropolitan–Vickers, carried out a study into the potential of submarine nuclear power. The Treasury approved £500,000 for this research although the study was eventually suspended when it became apparent that the available nuclear fuel would be required for the nuclear weapons programme. However, in 1954 the Atomic Energy Authority stated that the necessary fuel could be made available. As a result of this, the Naval Section at Harwell (Naval Cell), under Captain Harrison-Smith, was placed on a more formal footing and work began in earnest. During the year the staff were increased by personnel from the Royal Corps of Naval Constructors (RCNC) and engineers from Vickers–Armstrongs Limited. Despite this, British interest was primarily centred round the German-inspired Hydrogen Peroxide (HPT) Steam Turbine, which eventually went to sea in two Ex-class submarines, HMS *Excalibur* and HMS *Explorer*. At this time the Russians were about to deploy their own nuclear submarines. It was intended that the high-speed peroxide submarines would enable anti-submarine forces to gain experience in tracking and attaching high-speed underwater targets.

The proposal that a submarine, particularly a nuclear-powered submarine, would make an ideal missile launching platform was being investigated primarily in America; this idea was not original and history perhaps gives some clues to its origin. The Germans had fired artillery rockets from a launcher fitted to the deck of a U-boat in May/June 1942. It was found that the rockets could even be fired while the submarine was submerged. In order to attack America, it was proposed that a V2 missile could be stowed in a watertight container that would be towed to the American coast by a submarine. When the submarine arrived at its destination, tanks in the container would be flooded to bring it to the vertical and the missile would be launched. The project was given the code name Prufstand XII. During the early 1950s the Americans developed a similar idea with the Golem towed missile launcher.

In 1946 the US Bureau of Ordnance asked the Applied Physics Laboratory to update an existing project for a seaborne long-range missile launching system. This emerged as Triton; a ramjet-powered ship or submarine-launched missile. Mountbatten initially showed some interest in this project when he met Gates in July 1955. This was developed into Regulus, a ship or submarine-launched, nuclear-armed, turbojet-powered cruise missile, which was deployed by the US Navy from 1955 to 1964. It was first launched from a submarine in July 1953 (USS *Tunny*, a Second World War fleet boat, was modified to carry the missile). In 1958 two purpose-built Regulus submarines, USS *Grayback* and USS *Growler*, were launched and these were joined by the nuclear-powered USS *Halibut*. These submarines carried out forty Regulus strategic deterrent patrols between October 1959 and July 1964, when the Polaris submarines were deployed.

In November 1953, the Defence Research Policy Committee (DRPC), considered the possibility of arming the UK with long-range ballistic rockets. Naval Staff considered the proposals for naval deployment of such a weapon, and the various directorates stated their preferred options, which tended to support a ballistic missile launched from a submarine. The Director of Plans (D of P) commented that it would bolster the Navy's case if a submersible launching platform could be developed in conjunction with a 1,000-mile-range ballistic missile and advised that the necessary design work should be progressed as quickly as possible. Only the Director of Gunnery opposed the proposal, stating that a missile-launching submarine was undoubtedly in the realms of fantasy and could not be made operational for at least twenty years. Also, the Defence Research Policy Committee (DRPC) did not agree with the Navy and pointed out in their March 1954 draft report that the insurmountable technical problems with the proposed ballistic missile would delay it for many years, provided of course they could be resolved in the first place. Notwithstanding the opposition, naval staff continued to pursue the seaborne deterrent proposal, with Flag Officer Submarines, Rear-Admiral Fawkes, endorsing this course of action.

At the same time the Air Staff had begun to examine the possibility of a strategic bombardment missile and the Royal Aircraft Establishment at Farnborough developed this into Air Staff Requirement OR1139 (August 1955). This was to be a 'medium range' land-based rocket that would eventually materialise as Blue Streak.

Naval staff continued to examine the possibility of a sea-launched ballistic missile; at one stage they considered a sea-going version of the Blue Streak. This interest was supported and encouraged by the US Navy. Admiral Mountbatten, then the First Sea Lord, was very interested in these developments. He had been closely involved with the decision in 1955 by Admiral Arleigh Burke, the American Chief of Naval Operations, to develop a solid-fuelled ballistic missile that would be capable of being fired underwater from a submerged submarine. He also discussed the prospects with Thomas Gates, the American Under-Secretary of the Navy, in July that year.

Mountbatten was more than aware that the RAF's V bomber force, with its free-fall bombs and vulnerable airfields, could only provide a short-term deterrent solution and that the only plausible real solution was to place the ballistic missiles in submarines, which would be invulnerable and could strike anywhere in the world. Mountbatten thought that once the Government recognised that the Navy could provide an ideal mobile launching platform for missiles, everything would fall into place. At the time he appeared to be referring to the Sea Slug missiles that would arm the County Class Destroyers that would enter service in the early 1960s, but maybe he was looking towards the day when Britain's nuclear deterrent would have to be carried by a Navy submarine.

Mountbatten played a major role in developing the Navy's bid for Polaris. However, he had to moderate his enthusiasm when he became Chief of the Defence Staff (CDS) in 1959. The main reason for this was to allay the Air Staff's understandable reservations regarding his bias towards naval interests, although despite his efforts these suspicions remained. His successor as First Sea Lord, Admiral Sir Charles Lambe, and the Permanent Secretary, Sir John Lang did not share his passion for the Polaris system. Undoubtedly their misgivings reflected the differing opinions among serving naval officers. Regardless of these differences, the Admiralty continued playing the 'long game', quietly confident that the deterrent role would eventually be delivered by Royal Navy submarines.

The Admiralty, and for that matter the Army, viewed the RAF's V Bomber fleet with some anxiety. The RAF received extra funding and increased status that went with the responsibility of carrying the country's nuclear deterrent. The RAF argued that it alone could provide worldwide air cover, which persuaded the Government to decommission the Navy's aircraft carriers, and that only it could deliver the nuclear bomb anywhere in the world. The service also argued that even the Americans were at least ten years away from deploying a ship or submarine that was capable of launching a nuclear weapon. To counter this, and probably in an attempt to secure a slice of the multi-million-pound nuclear strategy budget, the Royal Navy proposed that small submarines (X craft) could plant a nuclear bomb in enemy harbours. This plan became known as Operation Cudgel and three submarines were built, HMS *Stickleback*, HMS *Minnow* and HMS *Sprat*, with the intention that they would carry a nuclear mine based on the Red Beard weapon. The Army proposed its own solution, a massive land mine, code named Brown Bunny. Neither of these proposals were completed.

At this time Commander Peter La Niece, the Staff Gunnery Officer to the British Joint Services Mission in Washington DC, received a copy of the Operational Requirement for a ballistic missile with a range of 1,500 miles that would be based on the American Army's Jupiter missile. It was intended that the missile would be developed between the two services. During November 1955 this plan was subsequently conveyed to England, where it would be fair to say it was received with some scepticism.

On 4 November 1955, the US Navy was informed that the Air Force did not wish to cooperate on producing an Intermediate Range Ballistic Missile (IRBM); this essentially meant that the US Navy would produce a solid fuel missile that could be launched from a submarine. Lord Mountbatten was in a meeting with his opposite number Admiral Arleigh Burke at Key West and expressed interest in the project, enquiring if the Royal Navy could be involved in some small way. It was then agreed that a Royal Navy officer should be seconded to the Polaris team.

On 17 November 1955 the Americans created the Special Projects Office. Its primary aim was to oversee the submarine-launched missile programme, and at this stage the Army was developing the missile itself. The proposed missile was 56ft long and some 9ft in diameter, it weighed 40 tons and used liquid oxygen as a propellant. This had to be stored at absolute zero (-180°C) to prevent it from evaporating and the missile would take approximately two hours to fuel, not ideal characteristics for a submarine system. By the end of the month the US Navy stated it intended to develop a long-range, solid-fuelled missile that would be capable of being launched from a submerged submarine. In doing so it would overcome the serious hazards, difficult logistics, handling, storage and design problems associated with liquid fuels.

Rear Admiral W. Raborn was appointed Director Special Projects Office on 5 December 1955 and was essentially told he could pick his own small team from naval officers and civil servants, and report directly to the Secretary of the Navy. On 19 December 1955 a formal Navy Fleet Ballistic Missile Requirement was released. As with the initial requirement, this document was passed to British naval staff in Washington and was duly sent to London. It was received in certain naval sections with even more cynicism than the original requirement.

During early 1956 the British were asked for any information they might have regarding problems with the use of liquid propellants on board Navy ships; the Sea Slug missile was liquid fuelled. The Americans also asked for information about the Clausen Rolling Platform, a 700-ton floating platform designed to roll and pitch, simulating a ship at sea, which was built at Aberporth for the Sea Slug trials. A similar platform was built at Cape Canaveral (now Cape Kennedy). By the end of the year, the solid propellant was advanced enough to enable the US Navy to seek formal approval for the development under the code name Polaris.

Also in 1956, during late August, Admiral Rickover USN visited the UK and toured various sites involved in the UK naval atomic energy programme. During this visit USN *Sea Wolf* (a prototype submarine with a liquid sodium-cooled reactor) developed a leak. A complicated code had been developed in order that information could be passed to the admiral without compromising security. Unfortunately, the admiral forgot the code, and not being well-known for his patience, finished up yelling down the phone 'Just tell me in plain English!' It was during this visit that he met Lord Mountbatten. The two men seem to have got on rather well and this, in part, might have influenced the 1958 US–UK Mutual Defence Agreement.

A measure of Admiral Rickover's importance to the British nuclear submarine programme can be gleaned from the Admiralty's brief to Harold Macmillan prior to the admiral's visit to Britain in February 1959. It concluded that while the British nuclear propulsion project had undoubtedly benefited from Admiral Rickover's participation, he was always guided by the terms of the bilateral agreement and this could sometimes be a hindrance. Rickover's insistence that things had to be done his way also caused problems but, apart from that, the note acknowledged that the British project greatly benefited from his involvement and would not have made the progress it did, as quickly, without his assistance. In the covering letter the First Lord, Lord Selkirk, felt the need to point out that Rickover was a complicated character who had chips on both shoulders. That aside, he was easily flattered and he could be quite sharp, and probably rude, in his remarks. He concluded by advising the Prime Minister that while he should show appreciation for what Rickover had done, he should temper his thanks.

Admiral Rickover wanted to be involved in the selection process for British naval officers before they were posted to nuclear submarines, similar to his approach in the US Navy, but luckily Mountbatten managed to talk him out of this. Interestingly, Rickover was finally retired from the US Navy on the direct orders of President Reagan in 1982, after sixty-three years of military service; he had been in charge of the American nuclear propulsion programme for thirty years.

Throughout this period British naval staff in Washington were regularly briefed by members of the Special Projects team. In early 1957 Commander John Coote (Submarine Staff Officer), Vice Admiral Geoffrey Barnard (CBNS) and Commander Peter La Niece (Staff Gunnery Officer) attended a brief that covered the whole scope of the Polaris project. The British team was told the Polaris project had adopted the same rationale used by companies involved in naval aircraft development in so much as all aspects of the project, the submarine, its weapon systems, its propulsion and all associate equipment were treated as one complete system, not a series of unrelated subsystems. The British team was also told of the modern management practices used by the project such as Programme Evaluation and Review Technique (PERT) and Critical Path Analysis. The purpose of these was to direct attention and resources to areas that were not going according to plan. The team was also told that the project fostered very close relationships with civilian contractors involved in the project.

During July 1957, the US Navy amended the programme brief to provide a missile with a 1,500-mile range that would be ready for operational evaluation by 1 January 1965. By the end of 1957 the AEC stated that the Polaris warhead development would meet the requirements by 1960. In response, the Special Projects Team affirmed that the programme should be hastened to deliver a complete weapon system with a 1,200-mile range missile by October 1960, for approximately the same cost. The 1,500-mile range missile would be provided later. In December 1957, the team was given the approval to complete the first submarine by 1960.

Several other projects were undertaken to assist the Polaris project, the USS *Compass Island* was converted to test navigational equipment; the Peashooter, an experimental missile launch tube, was constructed on a pier head at the San Francisco Naval Shipyard and trials had been carried out using compressed air. Later an underwater missile launch facility was built at the US Navy-owned San Clemente Island off the California coast.

The launch of the Russian Sputniks in October and November 1957 was a cause of some concern for Western nations. It showed that the Russians had developed a 'heavy lift' capability and now could launch nuclear bombs at America. Shortly after this, Sir Edwin Plowden (AEA) and Sir Richard Powell (MoD) visited Washington and during the ensuing discussions it was suggested that Britain could procure a complete nuclear submarine propulsion plant. In January 1958 the necessary legislation was introduced to the Senate. There was some opposition to this Amendment, but Admiral Rickover spoke in favour of the arrangement. It was then proposed that a British company would buy the plant from an American company and install it in a British-built submarine. This company was Rolls-Royce and Associates (a combination of Rolls-Royce Limited, Vickers-Armstrong (Engineers) Limited and Foster Wheeler Limited). President Eisenhower signed the necessary legislation on 22 July 1958. The reason why Rickover was so keen to help the British may be judged from a letter he wrote in late 1957, talking about his support for the exchange of technology. He wrote, 'I did this because of my feeling of urgency about the international situation, my admiration for the British and particularly my great liking for Admiral Mountbatten.'

The Americans had shown that submarines could provide a suitable launch platform for the British nuclear deterrent and in the autumn of 1957 the First Lord of the Admiralty, Lord Selkirk, had a meeting with the Prime Minister. Primarily Lord Selkirk intended to brief him on progress being made on the nuclear propulsion programme but he also took the opportunity to advise Harold Macmillan that the proposed nuclear submarines could launch nuclear ballistic missiles. Lord Selkirk obviously felt the time was right to put the Navy's case forward, despite the fact that Macmillan was known to be hostile to military expenditure. Many feared that Macmillan's attitude to military spending could threaten the entire nuclear-powered submarine project.

Lord Selkirk was an ardent supporter of the Polaris system, which might be considered a somewhat unpatriotic stance for a former RAF man. During November 1957, *The Times* published a cynical article about the proposed submarine-launched missile system. Lord Selkirk immediately wrote to the editor, Sir William Haley, suggesting he ran an article, penned by himself, which would stress the nuclear-armed submarine's mobility, invulnerability and ability to draw fire away from the homeland. He concluded that although a submarine capable of launching a ballistic missile would not be available for a number of years, the concept was beginning to affect strategic thinking and he was of the opinion that over time its influence would grow. The Prime Minister was unimpressed, and despite further arguments from Sir Edwin Plowden, the respected chairman of the UK Atomic Energy Authority, on the advantages of the missile-carrying submarine, he remained unconvinced.

Nevertheless, the Admiralty prepared a paper asserting the case for Polaris, which it hoped to present to the Defence Committee at some time in the future. The Navy's approach could be best summed up in a letter Lord Selkirk wrote to his predecessor, Lord Hailsham, in January 1958. In this, he emphasised that he was keen to keep the possibility of Polaris submarines in the minds of colleagues. He stressed the importance of not 'pushing' the project too much as the Air Ministry would regard the whole thing as a red herring while so many technical problems still remained to be resolved. He concluded that he was sure that by 1967 missile sites would be 'out of this island' and at sea in Royal Navy submarines. This 'out of this island' philosophy was a very powerful one. One of the arguments against Blue Streak was its vulnerability due to the known locations of its fixed launching sites. Also, there were the devastating effects a large nuclear strike would have on the relatively small British Isles. It was a fact not wasted on the Americans; Mountbatten's US Navy colleagues sent him a cartoon of a submarine bearing the legend 'Move deterrents out to sea where the real estate is free and where they are far away from me'.

In February 1958, Mountbatten set up a working group to evaluate the cost and development time of Polaris with that of Blue Streak and the V-bombers. Perhaps not surprisingly, the completed report recommended that the Chiefs of Staff should consider Polaris. At the same time the Minister of Defence, Duncan Sandys, requested a paper on the proposed Polaris submarines, and this was duly forwarded to the Ministers of Defence, Supply and Air. Predictably, the report was weighted in favour of the Polaris system. Sandys forwarded this to the Chiefs of Staff, asking for their views on the possibility of acquiring Polaris from the Americans. This report, along with competing proposals, extending the life of or replacing the V bomber force and Blue Streak, were assessed by the Joint Planning Staff. Needless to say, the Air Ministry challenged the Admiralty case, arguing that even a thirty-two-missile Polaris submarine (as was sometimes proposed) had no more striking power than a single Blue Streak missile, and would cost twenty times as much. The Admiralty replied that it had already given considerable attention to the introduction and upkeep of the proposed Polaris weapon system and the Air Ministry's concerns could be resolved.

The former Director-General of Weapons, Rear-Admiral Michael Le Fanu, conducted a study to identify what the Admiralty would have to do if it was required to man and run the Polaris force. The resultant report considered administrative and manning issues, and, very controversially, suggested a separate organisation be set up to oversee the introduction of the Polaris system – an Admiralty within the Admiralty. He also suggested an eight-boat squadron, although at various stages of drafting the report the number varied between three and ten. Regardless of the number, these submarines would carry out ninety-four-day patrols and four submarines would be on patrol at any one time. This report became known as the Le Fanu report and was the 'prudent staff work' often mentioned. Despite the Navy's efforts, at the end of the year Blue Streak was still the favoured weapon system, although the Admiralty had raised awareness of its disadvantages and cost.

Admiral Lambe, who succeeded Mountbatten as the First Sea Lord in May 1959, agreed with his predecessor's aims, although he tended to be more restrained in pursuing them. He felt that it would be better to wait until the Polaris system had been shown to be feasible before making the final case. He also thought it would be better to wait and see what impact the introduction of Polaris would have on the American Ship Submerged Nuclear (SSN) programme. He decided that a more prolonged cautious approach should be adopted; he felt it would be better if the Navy was pushed into the Polaris project rather than 'volunteer' for it. Selkirk agreed, advising the Navy to be ready to state its case at some time in the future.

Admiral Burke's overenthusiastic 'help' could be embarrassing, and more sceptical members of the Naval Staff thought – with some justification – that he failed to grasp the subtleties of the British situation. It was a view that was justified when, just after Mountbatten left to become CDS, a letter arrived and was duly opened by his successor, instead of being passed on to Mountbatten. Lambe replied with a curt warning that the deterrent was a politically complicated and tricky problem, and that if anybody became aware of how closely Mountbatten and Burke were working together on the project, it would seriously damage the Navy's hopes.

However confident the Navy felt, it was far from guaranteed that it would be asked to shoulder the deterrent role; there were two people who strongly opposed this and both were ardent supporters of Blue Streak. The first was the Minister of Defence, Duncan Sandys, not the most successful in his role, who had the knack of irritating the service chiefs. Unfortunately his belief in Blue Streak was absolute, and the Admiralty knew that he would do everything in his power to ensure that it was the deterrent of choice. The second was Sir Frederick Brundrett, Chief Scientific adviser to the MoD. This former head of the Naval Scientific Service argued that a solid-fuelled missile, the only credible choice for a submarine-launched deterrent, would be unlikely to combine the required lift power with the necessary range.

The Air Ministry's objections to Polaris were based on the limited number of warheads that could be delivered to the target, the limited power of these warheads and the weapon's limited accuracy and range. The Navy counted with claims over Blue Streak's accuracy, cost and the recognised vulnerability of its land-based launch sites.

The Navy's overriding priority was to prove that Polaris was a viable system and to this end the Americans supplied all the information required. When certain elements of the Polaris system were questioned in Whitehall, Admiral Burke and his team would ensure that all the information required to counter the attack was supplied as quickly as possible. To avoid any delays Burke ordered that all relevant material concerning Polaris should be sent directly to London.

At this time, it was claimed that Polaris was accurate to 3 nautical miles at extreme range. Of this, 1 mile was attributed to the missile and 2 miles to the positional and directional errors of the launching submarine. This, along with the smaller warhead, undoubtedly weakened the Navy's argument, but the Navy countered that the accuracy was acceptable and Jigsaw, the Joint Global War Study Group, considered a warhead yield of between half a megaton and 3 megatons was sufficient to achieve one-third destruction of a city with a circular error probability (CEP) of 3 miles. Also, it was British strategic doctrine that the need for precise accuracy was becoming less important, the underlying principle being that the aggressor must aim for his opponent's rocket sites, while the retaliator would aim for larger targets such as cities.

The Navy was convinced the case for Polaris was irrefutable; the launching submarine could sustain a threat against targets over a very wide geographic area. This in turn made it possible to reduce missile flight time as the launch point could be positioned relatively close to the designated target. This gave the enemy less time to respond, and countered the RAF misgivings about the missile range; the submarines were also very difficult to detect.

It was obvious that costs would play a major role in deciding which deterrent system would be chosen. The Admiralty estimated that the first submarine could be at sea in 1966, with the full complement of eight deployed by 1970, each carrying sixteen Polaris missiles, at a total cost of £400 million. This included a contribution to American R&D costs. Needless to say, Ministry of Defence officials were doubtful that the programme could be delivered within this price frame. They were also concerned whether the country's limited stocks of fissile material could maintain the project. They also commented on the Admiralty's estimate of the expected R&D contribution, which they thought was ridiculous. As a result the Admiralty reassessed its estimates, only to reduce them to £320 million; the reduction was achieved by dramatically revising warhead costs.

This provoked Sir Richard Powell, the MoD's Permanent Under-Secretary, to condemn the Admiralty estimates as 'very much on the low side', and he argued that they had underestimated the cost of warhead development. At the end of the day, he contended, there was little to choose, cost-wise, between the two systems.

Regardless of Sir Richard's attack, the Admiralty felt confident in their position; they had assurances from Admiral Burke that R&D costs would be waived and he was anticipating that the missiles would be provided at production cost. While this arrangement was undeniably appealing, the Admiralty was very conscious of the potential effects on other naval programmes and it was accepted that the Polaris system should not be allowed to have an impact on them. Additional resources would also have to be provided by central government so current plans and programmes would not be affected.

Another problem, in fact a potentially major stumbling block, was whether or not British shipyards had the capacity to build the proposed submarines while maintaining the SSN building programme. A meeting on 16 April 1959, chaired by Mountbatten, was entirely dedicated to the possible effects of such a programme, and the feasibility of building the Polaris submarines within a reasonable timescale without major disruption to other programmes was doubted. The possibility of increasing building capacity would have to be investigated before the Admiralty Board could consider 'whether or not they should continue the Polaris battle'.

It was during this period that Admiral Burke sent a signal to Mountbatten, or so it was rumoured, saying, 'For God's sake Dickie stop pestering me, put one of your men in our Special Projects Office (SPO) and he can tell you all you need to know.' As a result of this, in October 1958 the first Royal Navy liaison officer, Cdr H.M. Simeon, was appointed to the SPO as Special Projects Royal Navy (SPORN). He was fully integrated into the project team and was allowed to attend Admiral Raborn's Monday morning meetings, where progress of the Polaris programme was discussed. He was allowed full access to SPO reports and he reported all relevant facts back to

London, with the full approval of his American hosts. During his two-year stay in America he witnessed missile trials and visited most of the contractors involved in the project, being relieved by Commander W.J. Graham in early 1961. Simeon's next appointment was as Director Gunnery Division, but he was eventually reunited with the Polaris programme when he was appointed to Chief Polaris Executive (CPE) when it was formed in 1963.

The Conservative Defence Minister Duncan Sandys believed that future wars would be fought by missiles and high-flying nuclear-armed aircraft; his 1957 Defence Review was based on this conviction and it radically altered the armed forces. In the review he also took the opportunity to reorganise the aircraft industry, with smaller companies being merged into larger ones. Needless to say, this was a very unpopular move and the Government made matters worse by stating that it would only give contracts to the newly merged firms. The Army strength was reduced, with many regiments being amalgamated. Although the Navy escaped relatively unscathed, Sandys stated that 'the role of the Navy in a Global War is somewhat uncertain', not exactly a ringing endorsement of its future. This only added to the difficulty the defence chiefs had presenting a united front to Sandys; he was undoubtedly detested by all the service chiefs. In fact, the Chief of the Imperial General Staff (CIGS), Sir Gerald Templer is said to have argued with Sandys every time they met. Matters were not helped by the fact that the service chiefs had equally uncomfortable working relationships with one another. There was bitterness at the relationship between Lord Mountbatten and the Chief Scientific Officer, Sir Solly Zuckerman. Mountbatten shared a 'mutual loathing' with Sir Francis Festing, who was Field Marshal when he was CIGS. He was also distrusted by the Air Staff. All this was underpinned by inter-service rivalries, suspicions and resentments. In part this distrust and ill feeling was the reason why Sandys was determined to combine the separate military ministries into the one central Ministry of Defence; he hoped it would stop or at least reduce the squabbling between the service chiefs.

In early 1958 the First Lord of the Admiralty the Earl of Selkirk, Secretary of the Admiralty Sir John Lang and the Naval Secretary Rear Admiral Alistair Ewing visited Washington and were invited to a special Polaris briefing by Admiral Raborn. The offer was duly accepted, and a few days later the British visitors, accompanied by Commander La Niece, attended a brief in the Special Projects Office Management Centre (the Holy of Holies) given by Raborn himself. The wide-ranging presentation gave the visitors much food for thought; of particular interest was the fact that Raborn managed the budget for the project, an alien concept to the British Naval staff.

During this period Britain was developing Blue Streak, an RAF manned ICBM, and a joint US/UK Ballistic Missile Advisory Committee was formed. This committee also visited America and included visiting various companies involved in the Polaris Project: Lockheed, Aerojet General, etc. The committee seemed to view the whole set-up with a large degree of scepticism and general disbelief.

The Joint Planning Staff's review of the various deterrent options available to Britain failed to provide an answer and only highlighted already identified concerns, be they political or technical in nature. As a result of this, in January 1959 the issue was referred to the Chiefs of Staff Committee. They formed a small subcommittee whose members were to determine how the British contribution to the nuclear deterrent could be effectively maintained over the coming years. This subcommittee, which for some reason became known as Benders, was the formal forum where the supporters of the various deterrent options, be they airborne or submarine launched, could present their cases. The new committee's aims were to review whether or not there was an alternative to the British independent deterrent, and, if not, what the replacement system should be. These aims were decided at a meeting at Chequers, the Prime Minister's country residence, in a meeting attended by senior service officers and civil service chiefs but no other politicians apart from Prime Minister Harold Macmillan. It was claimed that this get together was to say goodbye to the retiring Chief of the Defence Staff. Needless to say, Sandys saw the committee as a threat to Blue Streak, managing to delay the start of the review until late July. Initially the committee chairman, Sir Richard Powell, the MoD's Permanent Under-Secretary, intended to exclude the Air and Naval chiefs primarily because he felt their opinions, understandably, would favour their own service. He revised this view once the terms of reference and membership were settled at the Chequers meeting and the services were to be represented by their vice-chiefs, Rear-Admiral Laurence Durlacher, Lieutenant General Sir William Stratton and Air Vice-Marshal Sir Edmund Hudleston. Other members were Sir Patrick Dean from the Foreign Office, Sir William Strath from the the Ministry of Supply, B.D. Fraser from the Treasury and Sir William Cook from the Atomic Energy Authority. Initially Powell wanted to exclude Sir Frederick Brundrett, Scientific Advisor to Minister of Defence, primarily because he was an ardent supporter of Blue Streak, but Sandys insisted he was included. To begin with, the committee set about defining what was the purpose of the deterrent and how its effectiveness could be measured. To be credible the members agreed that the deterrent should be capable of attacking, with ground-burst megaton weapons, the centres of thirty to forty major Russian cities, including Moscow, Leningrad and Odessa. Unlike previous plans, they decided that a high degree of accuracy was not required to achieve this, and this suited the supporters of Polaris.

In February 1960, the Defence Committee of the Cabinet, not unexpectedly, agreed to cancel Blue Streak, and also gave their formal approval to acquire the American air-launched Skybolt. As a result, when Macmillan visited President Eisenhower at Camp David in March 1960, he came back with Skybolt. This gentleman's agreement was very vague and those involved, on either side of the Atlantic, in putting it into force were at best confused about the scope and objectives of the agreement. Despite several attempts by Government officials to clarify matters the confusion remained. The RAF had been involved in the development of this missile, their own 'prudent staff work'.

Very few outside the Air Ministry believed in the viability of Skybolt, if it actually materialised. Certainly, from the naval viewpoint it would only be a stopgap, until the Government was forced to buy Polaris, if it wished to remain a nuclear power. Given the doubts about Skybolt, and the infirmity of the agreements, the Navy and its supporters pressed the case for Polaris more vigorously than before.

The new First Lord of the Admiralty, Lord Carrington, did not approve of the Camp David agreement and in the Defence Committee he argued that the better option would be to avoid Skybolt and, providing the Americans were willing, take the Polaris option. Conversely, Macmillan was of the opinion that the Government should not commit itself to either weapon system, although the minutes of the Defence Committee seemed to show that they considered Polaris only as a possible successor to Skybolt and not as a current option, although Carrington did challenge the accuracy of this. Sandys, who was now Minister of Aviation, was due to make a statement in the House of Commons. His draft statement implied that the RAF would get a new aircraft to carry Skybolt, essentially making Polaris redundant. Carrington objected, claiming that Sandys went beyond the Defence Committee agreement. He insisted that there should be no public statement committing the Government to Skybolt in advance of a further report assessing the future deterrent options from the British Nuclear Deterrent Study Group (BNDSG). He was unsuccessful.

Later in 1960 Carrington suggested that Britain should buy a small number of Polaris submarines from the Americans, as building them would only be economical if a larger number were to be built.

At the next meeting of the BNDSG, the argument was primarily between the supporters of a submarine force and those who wanted to see the continuation of the airborne deterrent. The argument seemed to be in favour of Polaris, with the Air Council being advised that Skybolt was not the favoured option.

Sir Solly Zuckerman chaired an independent expert group that was essentially a subcommittee of the BNDSG. This subcommittee consisted of independent scientists and in a rather blatant act of bias service chiefs were excluded, supposedly to avoid discussions sinking into an inter-service shouting match, as each side attempted to state its case without regard to any other arguments. The Air Staff insisted that the service chiefs and defence scientists should be included in the subcommittee membership and experts should be brought in as required. Eventually the Air Ministry scientific adviser was given a place on the subcommittee; the Admiralty scientific adviser had been a member from the initial meeting. This did little to allay Air Force suspicions of bias on the part of the chairman; in the committee only two members defended Skybolt – James Lighthill, who had recently been appointed director of the Royal Aircraft Establishment, Farnborough, and Hugh Constant, the Air Ministry scientific adviser.

Zuckerman strongly held the view that the RAF's V-bombers were essentially defenceless when compared with Polaris. This opinion was shared by most of the subcommittee members.

He repeatedly expressed doubts as to whether or not Skybolt was viable. This lead Constant to complain that the members of the group were, as a whole, prejudiced against Skybolt. He certainly seemed to have a point. Three of the non-ministry scientists had written a paper supporting the submarine-launched missile system; the Air Ministry officers dismissed this as a 'Polaris propaganda pamphlet'. One Air Ministry official was of the opinion that, regardless of the composition of the committee of experts examining future nuclear weapons systems, they would always start with a pro submarine bias. It would appear these concerns were well grounded; within six months the Air Council was informed that the Navy may well assume the nuclear deterrent role.

As the committee was compiling its report, Constant wrote a rather caustic account of the meeting; he stated that Zuckerman heckled and interrupted him continuously, making it impossible for him to state his case. He also pointed out that he and Lighthill were the only members not to vote for Polaris. Cockburn also tried to register his concerns but these were dismissed by Zuckerman.

Zuckerman made it clear that he would not allow the committee to reach anything other than a unanimous decision and that decision would be that Polaris was the favoured option. He blocked the draft report, which was worded to avoid reaching a decision between Polaris and Skybolt.

This action infuriated Lighthill, who accused Zuckerman of being blatantly biased, called his chairmanship of the group into question and questioned his professionalism and integrity. He claimed that Zuckerman had misused his position, attempting to influence the group by making remarks about the status of Skybolt that were largely unverified or mere rumours. Zuckerman was even accused of amending the draft report to show the committee were totally in favour of Polaris. As a result, Lighthill and Constant announced they would produce a minority report, highlighting the inaccuracies in the main report to show that, at best it was misleading and it failed to reflect the actual evidence presented to the group. Zuckerman was eager to resolve these issues within the expert group rather than have them aired in front of the full BNDSG. Initially he appeared to concede, arranging a further meeting at which compromises were made and a report agreed by all parties was signed.

It was an erroneous victory for the Skybolt campaigners; Zuckerman's carefully interpreted presentation of the agreed text to the full BNDSG meeting essentially disregarded the opposition, failing to mention the compromise. In the report he concluded that at least the majority of the committee were in favour of the submarine-launched deterrent. Air Vice-Marshal Huddleston, the Vice-Chief of Air Staff, challenged this claim but he was a little too late to affect the outcome; the BNDSG had before it a paper recommending further investigation of the Polaris missile system.

At the end of 1961 there was no official decision as to whether or not Polaris or Skybolt should be the nuclear deterrent. The Air Ministry was content with this, thinking the longer it took to reach a decision, the more time Skybolt would have to prove itself. The Admiralty was equally comfortable with this position and for the same reason; the longer it took to reach a decision the longer the Americans had to prove the feasibility of Polaris. The Navy also cleverly managed to avoid the critical and fundamental political argument; Skybolt came virtually without political strings, whereas the Americans would only make Polaris available if it was assigned to NATO. The Admiralty presented the two weapons systems as politically equivalent.

Skybolt was cancelled by the Americans in December 1962, so the only alternative to abandoning the UK contribution to the Western deterrent would be to arrange a deal over Polaris. The American decision might have suited Macmillan; he was trying to reduce the number of nuclear warheads held by Britain and the proposed Polaris submarines would require fewer warheads than the RAF's V bomber force. In the same month, President Kennedy and Macmillan signed the Nassau Agreement, which in the broadest terms said America would supply Polaris missiles and their associated systems to Britain. Britain would supply the nuclear missile warheads and the submarines that would launch the missiles. The British started on the project before Christmas and press releases were put out almost immediately; the credibility of the Conservative Government depended on a credible nuclear policy and the overriding need was to appoint someone to head the project, a team leader.

Also during this period there were discussions in the BNDSG regarding the possibility of basing a small number of Polaris submarines east of Suez. In 1963 the objective was to get the project started, so it was decided to delay any basing decision for two years. After two years it was decided to wait a further two years. In early 1966 a decision had to be made and a paper was commissioned. The paper highlighted several potential problems, a shore base or specially converted depot ship would be required. Also, navigational aids and survey work would be required in the Indian Ocean. The report suggested Singapore, Fremantle or an Indian Ocean island.

The man chosen to head the British Polaris project was Sir Hugh Stirling Mackenzie KCB DSO★ DSC, who was serving as Flag Officer Submarines at the time. He received a telephone call from the First Sea Lord, Admiral Sir Caspar John, on 28 December 1962 asking if he would consider heading the Polaris project, although he would 'twist his arm until he would bloody well scream' if he chose not to take the offered job. He was given the weekend to think about it and was invited to give his answer at a meeting the following Monday. Sir Hugh's answer was yes and he was appointed Chief Polaris Executive (CPE), whose sole objective was to set up the organisation that would get Polaris into service within five years. In this role he was responsible to the Controller of the Navy (Vice Admiral Michael Le Fanu) for delivering the Polaris project on time and to cost. Such was the importance attached to the project that if he required assistance he had direct access at any time to any member of the Board of Admiralty.

It would be a project of unimaginable scale and scope. The as yet non-existent organisation would have to arrange the building of the submarines and their support facilities, crews would have to be trained, etc. The next day, New Year's Day 1963, Admiral Mackenzie found himself in an office on the ground floor of the North Block of the Admiralty Building with only a desk and a chair, even the phone wasn't connected. There was no staff and no paperwork. It was not the most reassuring of starts.

Mackenzie faced many problems in the early days of the project, aside from the lack of suitable office furniture, not least of which was the Polaris Agreement itself. Most agreements are signed after weeks, if not months, of detailed negotiations by people directly concerned with the project. In this case the reverse was true. The agreement was signed outlining, in the very broadest terms, what the outcome would be, so one of the first tasks was to actually detail how the terms of the agreement would be met by both sides. It took several months before a workable agreement was reached. Issues that needed to be addressed and clarified included how the payments would be made and what would Britain be paying for, and apart from the obvious hardware costs, how would the information exchange be costed? The Americans had argued that the British orders for equipment should be tied into American orders as the larger amounts would present cost benefits to both countries. Britain argued that this would mean that the American programme would have priority and equipment might be delivered before it was required, thereby incurring unplanned expenses as there might be storage costs until the equipment was actually required.

Mackenzie had some understanding of the American Polaris Project; the previous year on a routine visit to Washington he had been given a very comprehensive brief by Rear Admiral I.J. Galantin, the Director of Special Projects, detailing the procedures used within the SPO to keep the project 'on track'. He also had at hand the Le Fanu report, the 'prudent piece of staff work' prepared by Admiral Le Fanu some three years previously, which detailed the organisation that would be required to bring Polaris into service within the Royal Navy.

One of the first tasks, using the Le Fanu report as a guide, was to fill the key posts within the organisation. Supported by the Controller and the Secretary of the Admiralty (Clifford Jarrett), within a few days personnel, both civilian and naval, were appointed to posts within the fledgling organisation.

One area where there was a potential for trouble was the production of the nuclear warheads. The responsibility for this lay with the Atomic Weapons Research Establishment and the Ministry of Aviation. The latter claimed they had statutory for all missiles and should have total responsibility for the Polaris project, a view strongly supported by the Minister of Aviation, Julian Amery. The Navy's argument that the submarines along with their navigation, control and missile launch systems should be treated as a complete single weapon system was finally accepted after much diplomatic effort by the First Lord. To save face, a Polaris Project Office was set up in the Ministry of Aviation headed by Rear Admiral F. Dossor; he would have responsibility to both the Minister of Aviation and CPE for the design and production of the warheads and the re-entry system. The Navy retained the responsibility for the procurement, fitting and maintenance of the missiles themselves and their associate support systems.

During the first week, the principal positions within the organisation had been agreed by the Admiralty and such was the importance and urgency attached to the project, many of them were already filled. It quickly became apparent the sheer size and immense scope of the project would cause countless problems, be they about security or liaison with the Americans. At this stage, the Polaris Agreement was far from a workable document; dealing with other Admiralty departments and coordination with other Government departments including the Treasury, Foreign Office, Ministry of Public Works and Ministry of Aviation had to be addressed urgently. Also, where would the fledgling organisation be based, Bath or London? Office space needed to be found for the rapidly expanding team, funding needed to be secured, and decisions needed to be made about who was going to build the submarines and how the contracts would be handled. This was made all the more difficult as at this early stage it had not been decided how many submarines would be required, how many missiles they would carry or where they would be based.

On 8 January a team flew to Washington led by Sir Solly Zuckerman, the Government's Chief Scientific Advisor. It included Vice Admiral Varyl Begg (Vice Chief of Naval Staff), CPE and various other representatives from the

Ministry of Aviation. One result of the meetings with SPO was the setting up of the Joint Steering Task Group (JSTG), which would ensure that both the American and British programmes advanced in tandem and British requirements were not lost in the hustle and urgency of the American programme. During the three-day, very busy visit they discussed the number of missiles each submarine would require and weather the A2 or A3 version of the missile would be supplied. While obviously crucial to the British programme, these decisions would also have an impact on the American programme.

Arriving back in his office on 14 January, CPE found that the Dreadnought Project Team had been transferred to his organisation. This team, under the leadership of Sir Rowland Baker, had been set up under the Director General Ships (Sir Alfred Sims) to design and oversee the building of HMS *Dreadnought* at Vickers in Barrow-in-Furness. This was Britain's first nuclear-powered submarine, although the reactor was supplied by the Americans. While this was a welcome move as it showed the beginning of acceptance of CPE by other Admiralty departments, he was far from out of the woods. There were still disagreements about the design of the submarines; whether or not the submarines should carry eight or sixteen missiles and whether or not these missiles should be the A2 or A3 variant. The Americans were in favour of sixteen missiles and warned that any other configuration would incur considerable costs as a great deal of redesigning would be required. The Americans were also in favour of the A3 missile. Even though it was still undergoing tests, they were confident that it would be successful, and they intended to stop production of the A2.

On 17 January Admiral Galantin visited London as part of a series of meetings between the two project teams and to confirm the need for a further agreement, essentially to clarify the Nassau Agreement. This would cover the exact terms regarding the supply and maintenance of the missiles and all their associated equipment; the supply of the relevant technical information, what measures were required for insuring mutual progress and priorities between the two programmes, and how and when payments would be made. Before he left, an outline plan had been evolved detailing how these issues would be addressed.

Another problem Mackenzie had to deal with during this initial period was the fact that he was, for all intents and purposes, still Flag Officer Submarines, and his sudden disappearance from Fort Blockhouse caused some confusion as his new appointment was not widely known. This appears to have been due to the ongoing argument with the Minister of Aviation. By the third week in January the admiral's appointment in his new role of CPE had been made public and he could finally concentrate on his primary role; the Government required Polaris to be operational in 1968 and the responsibility for this lay entirely with the Polaris Executive.

Mackenzie set up his headquarters in London, within the Admiralty. He was supported by a small staff that included R.N.P. Lewin, who was Chief Administrative Officer; he was an Assistant Secretary from the Admiralty and so provided much-needed experience in dealing with other Government departments. His assistant was P. Naylor, who went on to succeed him in 1966. Also on the staff was Captain R. McKaig, who was later to become Deputy CPE. He had been the then Captain Mackenzie's commander when he had been the commanding Officer of HMS Ganges, the boys' training establishment on the Suffolk coast, in 1958. Commander J.R. Grimwood, the admiral's secretary when he was FOSM, also transferred to the fledgling organisation. On 6 February 1963 the Admiralty issued an 'Office Memorandum' that essentially legitimised CPE's organisation, established its authority and laid down its terms of reference. On the same day CPE issued the first project programme, Longcast No. 1. Two days later CPE issued his 'mission statement': 'To deploy on station the first RN Ballistic Submarine with its missiles, and with fully report, in July 1968 and thereafter the remainder at six monthly intervals. These dates cannot be allowed to slip.'

The initial cost estimates for the project were:

	£m
4 Polaris submarines	141
Other shipbuilding costs	9
Support costs	47
Missiles and torpedoes	85
R & D	52
US overhead costs	6
UK headquarters costs	5
Estimated total cost	345

During the same period the Dreadnought Project Team, which had been handed over to CPE, stationed at Bath was undergoing a similar rapid expansion. Under its leader, Rowley Baker, his title of DPT was retained but in the new organisation stood for Director Polaris Technical. In his developing organisation Sidney John Palmer RCNC was responsible for submarine design and construction; Captain C.W.H. Shepherd was to oversee the procurement, installation and upkeep of the Polaris weapon system; and Captain L.D. Dymoke and H.C. Fitzer were responsible for the submarines' nuclear propulsion plant and electrical systems. While they were all experts in their fields they were breaking new ground and the systems destined for the Polaris programme were completely new to the Navy. HMS *Dreadnought*, with her American-supplied reactor, was still fitting out at Barrow; the British reactor that would power the Polaris submarines was still undergoing trials at Dounreay and was some months away from being fitted into HMS *Valiant*, which was still building at Barrow.

In February 1961, a small team of professional officers visited America to appraise the Polaris programme. They visited the various factories and facilities involved in the project and were very impressed with the open and friendly attitude of the Americans. The visit was arranged by Lord Mountbatten. Perhaps as an omen of things to come, during this visit two Skybolt test firings failed, much to the delight of their American hosts, who were all from the Polaris Special Project team. In his summary of visit Palmer wrote that Britain should build five Polaris submarines, and these should be based on the Valiant design with the missile compartment inserted in the middle. The US missile compartment was 1ft in diameter smaller than the Valiant pressure hull. He reasoned that it would be difficult, at best, to change the layout of the American missile compartment, and the problems could be overcome by adding a small compartment, about 20ft long, between the British reactor compartment and the American missile compartment. And so AMS 2 was born/conceived. This summary became known as the Palmer report. Interestingly, the report went on to say that the five submarines should be based at Devonport and the armaments depot should be sited at Ernsettle, just outside Plymouth on the banks of the Tamar.

Rowley Baker also faced many of the same problems Mackenzie had in London, such as the recruitment of suitably qualified people (not the easiest of tasks considering the novel nature of the undertaking), and appropriate office accommodation. Drawing offices had to be found, and because of the sensitive nature of the task, these had to be physically secure. Also, all the newly recruited staff had to have the necessary security clearances.

Learning from the American experience, Mackenzie introduced what were then innovative management procedures, such as Critical Path Analysis, Programme Evaluation and Review Technique (PERT) and Programme Management Plans (PMPs). He felt that these techniques would allow him to control and track this vast programme. The admiral's preference for these newfangled management tools were by no means shared by his colleagues in the Admiralty and the traditional British shipbuilding industry. A great deal of time was spent by CPE and his staff during these first few months explaining to the appropriate people in Whitehall and industry the necessity of using these techniques to the successful completion of the project.

CPE's way forward became slightly clearer when in January 1963 it was finally decided that the submarine would carry sixteen missiles. Finally in-depth design work could begin, potential shipbuilders could be approached and consideration could be given to ordering 'long lead time' equipment. Now that it was known how many missiles each submarine would carry, it was relatively easy to agree that four submarines would be built and delivered at six-monthly intervals. The Government retained the option of building a fifth submarine. Once the question of how many missiles should be carried had been answered, it had to be decided who would build the submarines. This heralded a period of heated disagreements and lobbying. Vickers at Barrow was the only yard in the UK with nuclear build experience and as such was obviously the yard of choice. Indeed, Vickers offered to build the four proposed submarines but as it neither had the capacity nor resources to build all of them to the required timescale an additional yard would have to be found. Cammell Laird at Birkenhead and Scotts at Greenock, which both had experience of building conventional submarines, were considered. The Birkenhead yard was finally chosen as it was felt that it would be easy to upgrade and enlarge the facilities, particularly the building slipways. It was decided that Vickers would build boats one and three and Cammell Laird would construct two and four. Vickers was to be the 'lead yard' and as such would supply Lairds with all the required diagrams and information. This arrangement caused numerous problems, the majority of which were caused by the lack of suitably qualified personnel, and Rowley Baker and his staff spent a great deal of time maintaining friendly relationships between the two yards.

On 19 February 1963 CPE left for Washington with a large team of Admiralty and Ministry of Aviation personnel to clarify and validate the Nassau Agreement. This resulted in the Polaris Sales Agreement, which achieved extremely good terms for Britain, primarily due to the negotiating efforts of Jim Mackay, Deputy Secretary (G) in the Admiralty. The agreement was signed by both governments on 6 April 1963. It formalised the already extensive cooperation between the two Polaris project teams. It also allowed Vickers and the Electric Boat Company and other contractors to exchange information. Despite this relatively relaxed environment of information exchange, the mercurial Admiral Rickover would not allow any exchange of information regarding the nuclear power plant.

CPE returned to London on 2 March 1963, some weeks before the negotiations were due to finish, but he felt they were going well and his time would be better spent in his office tending to the many problems that still needed to be addressed. Among them was getting the two shipbuilders and Rolls-Royce and associates into the dialogue; even at this stage the time for ordering 'long lead' items was running out. It still had to be decided what missile (A2 or A3) the submarines would carry. The Ministry of Aviation was delaying the decision and CPE felt the Polaris Programme should have its own 'cell' within the ministry and that relationships between the two organisations had to be improved at all costs. Both the Polaris Executive and the Technical Directorate, even at this early stage, needed to be expanded to take into account the vast management, logistic and design effort that would be required to provide a base with all the necessary support and maintenance for the submarines and their crews. It would also be necessary to build an armaments depot to maintain the missiles and their nuclear warheads.

With this in mind it would also be necessary to mount a large PR campaign to counter all the adverse publicity the programme was generating along with the general 'ban the bomb' movement. Just this part of the programme was a vast undertaking that required the collaboration between several Admiralty departments, the Ministry of Public Building and Works, the local authorities, the Health and Safety Executive, Scottish Department, Ministry of Transport and numerous other agencies. Only by using the new management techniques was CPE able to control and monitor this vast, diverse group. To help deal with this, Rowley Baker's Technical Directorate was expanded to include the Polaris Logistics Officer (PLO), who would be responsible for dealing with these matters. There was some considerable argument about whether the PLO should be a naval officer or a civilian. Eventually CPE won the day when in May the recently retired Captain L. Bomford was appointed to the post.

CPE was of the opinion that the Polaris submarines would require a dedicated base. The Admiralty agreed with this decision, although the Government was slow in giving its approval. This base would be Faslane on the Clyde. Several ministries didn't share this view; the Treasury, the Ministry of Transport and even the Ministry of Defence thought the missile submarines should be based at Rosyth. They also expressed concerns about the potential dangers the base would pose to the emergency oil fuel depot at Garelochhead. Admiral Mackenzie argued that Faslane should be developed as a base for both the Fleet submarines and the Polaris submarines. With Admiralty backing, approval was finally given for a new base that would have the necessary jetties, workshops, training facilities, accommodation and the necessary married quarters. Approval was also given to build an armaments depot at Coulport on Loch Long, adjacent to the Gareloch. There was a great deal of unrest amongst the local community and CPE and his staff spent a great deal of time and effort on quelling these fears. The previous year, in response to the Palmer report, FOSM Sir Arthur Hezlet suggested that the proposed Polaris submarines should be based in an underground harbour. The submarines would approach the base submerged and settle on to a trolley, which would then be pulled into the base. Construction work was started at the Faslane site in March 1962, with the Polaris School one of the first buildings to be built.

A cloud appeared on the horizon when, in April 1962, the Secretary of State for Defence, Peter Thorneycroft, suggested that Admiral Mackenzie should be replaced by a civilian. The gentleman he had in mind was Dr Beeching, of British Rail fame. Luckily the Sea Lords fiercely opposed this proposal and Mackenzie remained in post. This episode seems to have caused CPE to reflect on whether or not there was any value in bringing in business expertise; the recently retired chairman of Schweppes, Sir Fredrick Hooper, was brought in to advise. In general, he confirmed that the CPE's planning and management strategy were sound and there was no need for changes. Unfortunately, Sir Fredrick died before the end of the year but even in that short amount of time Mackenzie felt he made a great contribution.

During January 1963, SPO Admiral Galantin had suggested setting up a joint working group, which would meet at regular intervals to ensure that the two projects ran smoothly and priorities did not clash. This materialised as the Joint Steering Task Group (JSTG), which held its first meeting in June 1963. The meetings were initially held quarterly, then moved to four-monthly. Apart from dealing with potential conflicts, the JSTG also dealt with matters relating to the interpretation of the Polaris Sales Agreement and its supporting technical arrangements. This arrangement worked so well that in 1993 the Working Group was used to negotiate the Trident introduction. The work of the Steering Group was supplemented by two exchange officers: Captain Peter La Niece was seconded to the SPO in Washington and Captain P. Rollings USN in London. Due to ill health, the latter was replaced by Captain Hamilton and was eventually succeeded by Captain W.P. Murphy. These two officers ensured there was close liaison between the two programmes and things ran smoothly; they were essential, especially during the early months, in laying the solid foundations that would see the programme through to a successful conclusion.

Within the Admiralty a committee was set up to help coordinate the efforts between all the various Whitehall departments and naval sections involved. Initially known as the Polaris Committee, it later became the Polaris Policy Committee.

By May 1963 the scale of the Polaris programme had become clearer. It was essential that the first British reactor was proven at sea. This was to be installed in HMS *Valiant*, which was building in Barrow. It seemed sensible to CPE that the SSN building programme, which was under the control of Director General Ships, should be transferred to CPE. It would allow him to avoid or manage conflicts in the two building streams and CPE had all the nuclear submarine designing and building knowledge and experience within his organisation, Rowley Baker's DPT.

On 21 May 1963, the Government placed orders for the Polaris submarines and the major works began at Faslane a day later. The final design for the submarine was agreed by summer 1963 and essentially frozen. CPE insisted that there would be no further alterations or additions to the submarines unless they addressed safety concerns or were the result of trials on HMS *Valiant*. CPE felt it was vital that all four submarines should be exactly the same; he argued that this was the only way the challenging timescales detailed in 'Longcast 63' could be met. (The initial forecast, Longcast 1, had been amended a number of times to reflect changing program needs.) This seemingly sensible policy was challenged on several occasions. Very early on in the programme the Director of the Compass Division strongly argued that a British designed and built ship inertial navigation system should be used instead of the American-supplied one. CPE was adamant that the weapon system, in total, should remain unchanged. Eventually, the argument was won and the American system remained intact.

A second case came to light in late 1966 when it was discovered that there was a difference of 1in in the length between bulkheads in the torpedo compartment of HMS *Renown*, the first Cammell Laird submarine, and the lead submarine HMS *Resolution*, but luckily this caused no significant problems. However, this was a particularly worrying discovery at the time as it pointed to a negligence in compliance with, or interpretation of, the controlling documents and drawings. This did not bode well for CPE's reliance on management techniques. While the two shipbuilding yards involved in the project were undoubtedly experts in conventional and traditional shipbuilding methods, they had yet to adopt the new management measures and techniques CPE was advocating if programme deadlines were to be met and the required quality standards achieved. The yards involved were slow to come on board but perhaps the turning point came in December 1963, when it became apparent that there were several failings in the programme and dates were slipping. A meeting was arranged between CPE, DPT and the managing director of Vickers, Leonard Redshaw. The meeting was far from friendly and at one stage Redshaw accused CPE of being 'only a bloody amateur who knew nothing of shipbuilding'. While undoubtedly true, Redshaw knew little about or chose to ignore the modern management procedures that the Polaris programme demanded. Peace was restored the following day when it was pointed out to Admiral Mackenzie that a horse called Polaris Missile was owned and ridden by an amateur. CPE sent a telegram to Mr Redshaw stating: 'Please note that the 4:30 at Newcastle yesterday was won by Polaris Missile owned trained and ridden by a bloody amateur'. It was received in the spirit it was sent and relationships between CPE and Vickers were greatly improved.

By the summer of 1963 several major elements of the programme had been decided and agreed, not least of which was the design of the submarines and the location of the submarine base. However, there were still countless issues to be addressed. Where would the manpower be found to crew the submarines and the ever-expanding departments of CPE and DPT, and could this be contained within the budget? How should the submarines be manned, one or two crews, what training would these crews require, and where would this training be conducted? On top of this, CPE was very concerned about the general lack of understanding about the project within the Admiralty and Government, particularly the demands it would make and the urgency required to meet the timescales. To rectify this, a series of presentations titled 'Polaris and its Management' were given to the appropriate departments.

During the second half of 1963 CPE and his staff were particularly concerned with issues involving the operational deployment of Polaris; from 1970 onwards it was intended that it would be the country's only deterrent. CPE had argued from the start of the programme that there should be five submarines in the fleet. With four submarines, one would always be at sea on deterrent patrol and they could just meet the necessary alongside periods for maintenance and refits and refuelling. CPE felt this was unsound and there was no leeway if a submarine had a major problem or accident. The argument continued for many months and was not finally resolved until the newly elected Labour Government cancelled the fifth submarine. Up until then CPE assumed that the fifth submarine would be ordered and 'long lead time' items where ordered, often referred to as 'contingency spares' to avoid any awkward questions from the Treasury.

Two other issues needed to be resolved before the end of 1963; the first was to decide the scope and purpose of the Royal Navy Polaris School (RNPS). This was to be built at Faslane and it was essential to the programme that it was operational one year before the first Polaris patrol. However, should the school be for training and instruction only or should it include test and instrumentation facilities? After discussions with the Americans it was decided that it should only be a school. Work started on the school on 3 January 1964 and it opened on 30 June 1966. In June 1964 the Ministry of Works announced that the Armaments Depot for the Polaris missiles would be built at Coulport. Training was also arranged in America at the US Polaris School at Dam Creek, Virginia, for the naval officers and ratings who would man the RNPS and the first British Polaris submarine.

The second issue was the design and construction of a floating dock that could lift a Polaris submarine and would be in place at Faslane by mid 1967. The dock, AFD 60, was built by Portsmouth Dockyard, delivered on time and worked satisfactorily for its entire working life, before being retired and sold to a firm in Iceland in the late 1990s.

At the beginning of 1964, although there were still a large number of problems to be resolved, CPE felt confident that the task was at least manageable. The modern management techniques coupled to the fortnightly progress meetings enabled CPE and his staff to closely monitor the progress of the project and allocate resources as required. During the preceding year Whitehall had slowly recognised and accepted the existence of CPE's organisation and collaboration between them improved immeasurably. Within the Admiralty, the Department of the Director General, Weapons (DWG), who had responsibility for navigation and communications systems, still insisted that the British Ships Inertial Navigation Systems (SINs) should be incorporated into the Polaris weapons system, regardless of the potential severe interface complications. Regular liaison meetings between DWG and CPE helped reduce the tension between the two organisations. Regular meetings were also held with the Atomic Weapons Research Establishment: there were problems in agreeing on the warhead design criteria and these were further compounded by staff shortages. At times these problems jeopardised the whole project and had the potential to delay the operational deployment of the first Polaris submarine in 1968.

At this time the building of the first two submarines was progressing well at Vickers and Cammell Laird, and both yards were expanding rapidly to enable them to cope with the demands of the programme. There was, however, one cloud on the horizon: the QT35 steel that was used in the construction of the submarine pressure hulls was in short supply. There were very few British steel makers who could produce the metal and even fewer that could work to the higher quality standards that the programme required. Another complication was that the molybdenum that was required to produce the steel was in very short supply. America normally supplied this, but due to its submarine building programme it had little to spare. CPE had to find an alternative source and it took a few very anxious weeks before another supplier was found: the Soviet Union.

Also during the first few months of 1964, Mackenzie made a series of visits to the steel makers and heavy engineering firms involved with the programme, primarily to acquaint himself with the problems they faced and also to impress on them the urgency of the programme and the need for high standards of quality control and planning. Additionally CPE and his team had to mount a concerted PR effort to counter various press reports and address the general lack of knowledge about the nation's deterrent in general and Polaris in particular. CPE also felt it necessary to respond to the generally ill-advised arguments from the Campaign for Nuclear Disarmament (CND).

Yet another cause for concern was the forthcoming General Election; Labour had made no secret of its opposition to nuclear weapons and had stated that if it won the election it would renegotiate the Polaris Agreement or cancel the programme altogether.

On 26 February 1964, about a year after the project started, the keel for the first Ship Submersible Ballistic Nuclear (SSBN) was laid at the Vickers yard at Barrow, but it was not quite the normal keel-laying ceremony in this case. A 250-ton section of the pressure hull was moved from the welding bay in the massive construction shed to the slipway where eventually it would be joined by the other sections required to build the submarine. Also on the same day, the Government finally approved the building of the fifth Polaris submarine.

As if CPE didn't have enough on his plate, in April 1964 the three separate armed service ministries were combined into a new organisation, the Ministry of Defence. Despite the turmoil caused by the move across Whitehall from the old Admiralty Building to the new MoD main building, there were several advantages. At last CPE had ample dedicated office space and conference facilities, security was much improved and his team finally got its own teleprinter network. As an added bonus, Mackenzie got his own official car; before this he had been using public transport. On the downside, the new organisation made getting things done more difficult for CPE; in the old Admiralty organisation he had direct access to the 'board'. Now the path was longer and certainly more tortuous.

The keel for the second Polaris submarine was laid at Cammell Laird on 26 June 1964, exactly on time as detailed in the Longcast. A shortage of suitably qualified specialised welders who could work with the QT35 steel used for the submarine hulls caused concern. This was only partially relieved after a nationwide recruiting campaign. Added to this was a series of strikes or threatened stoppages that jeopardised the overall programme. Also, CPE felt that the fitting out of *Valiant* was not progressing satisfactorily and the shipyard needed to allocate more manpower to the task. There was no easy solution to this, the specialised skills required to meet the very high cleanliness and quality standards that were required in both the SSBN and SSN build programmes were in short supply. A great deal of time and money was expended on rectifying this problem.

Within a few days of the General Election on 15 October 1964 CPE and his staff gave a presentation on the Polaris programme to the victorious

Labour ministers who might have any involvement with the Polaris programme. Among them was Denis Healey, the newly appointed Secretary of
State for Defence. Although CPE did not receive the hostile reception he
had been expecting, the Labour Party had made no secret of its opposition
to the project prior to the election, pledging that it intended to renegotiate
the Polaris Arrangement or cancel the project outright. However, no decision
was forthcoming. When Healey first examined the 'accounts', he could not
believe the cost of Polaris; he could not understand why it was so cheap. He
also recalls that certain senior naval officers expected him or actively encouraged him to cancel Polaris. They told him that although two submarines were
laid down, they could be converted to hunter-killer submarines at no extra
cost. Wilson told Healey not to brief the Cabinet as he intended to continue
with the Polaris project on the grounds that the financial penalties would be
colossal if the Government cancelled at this stage.

By mid November both shipyards were reporting that the political
uncertainty was causing key workers to leave the project. Regardless of the
Government's dithering, work continued on major parts of the project, the
proposed home port for the submarines at Faslane and the armaments depot
at Coulport. Suitable terms of reference and pay had to be agreed for the
Coulport staff, many of whom would be very highly qualified technicians
the likes of whom had not been seen in the civil service. They were men
who would soon be undergoing training on the new systems in America;
these would require the necessary increases in pay to allow for the higher
cost of living in that country. In both these cases the Treasury was not particularly helpful and CPE was involved in long and difficult discussions.

After a weekend at Chequers at the end of the year, at which defence
matters were top of the agenda, the Government announced it intended
to keep Polaris as the national deterrent, although it failed to mention the
size of the force. For CPE this meant that the programme was to remain
as it was and the first submarine was to be operational by mid 1968, with
the remainder following at six-monthly intervals. The Government finally
seemed to have grasped the enormity of the task when in early 1965 the
Minister for the Navy, when announcing the naval estimates, acknowledged
that the Polaris project was the most challenging peace-time task the Navy
could have been given.

In January 1965, CPE addressed a meeting of the Defence Council chaired
by the Secretary of State for Defence. He stressed that five submarines were

required to ensure that one would always be available on patrol. He also stressed that he felt that five submarines would not overstretch the crews or the personnel required to maintain the submarines; morale was a very important factor in the admiral's eyes. After his presentation, CPE was thanked by Healey but was told that his views were largely immaterial. The Treasury had demanded that the Polaris force be cut to three submarines, but after a meeting between the Cabinet's Overseas Policy and Defence Committees a compromise was reached and it was agreed that the force should consist of four.

As a result of this all, work and contracts associated with the fifth submarine were cancelled. Where contracts could not be cancelled the parts concerned became spares.

One has to agree with Mackenzie, who was never convinced that the cancellation was a Treasury-driven decision. He felt that it was a move to appease the left wing of the Labour Party, and it had the potential to have a detrimental effect on crew welfare. He later wrote: 'All that their (the Labour Party) clamour achieved was to lay an almost intolerable burden on the men, and the women, responsible for the efficiency of the deterrent.'

Finding the manpower to crew the new submarines was going to be a major problem because many of the posts would require highly specialised technicians. This would require a 40 per cent increase in submarine manpower during the mid 1960s, not the easiest of tasks as Healey was busily reducing the overall naval manpower by 10 per cent. Although there were many volunteers for the Polaris Squadron from both serving submariners and general service to meet the growing requirement, for the first time since the Second World War personnel were drafted into the Submarine Service. The number of volunteers had remained remarkably constant from the 1950s at around 450. While this number could meet the requirements of the conventional submarine squadrons and the rapidly expanding nuclear fleet. Also, new accommodation blocks at HMS Dolphin were built.

With the election out of the way and the project, admittedly now a smaller project, the future was secure and life in the CPE became more routine. All the major requirements of the programme were identified, milestones were defined and work was progressing well on building the submarines and their new base on the Clyde. Admiral Mackenzie and his team now found themselves monitoring progress and, although not everything ran smoothly, the management systems that were put in place highlighted areas of concern and allowed them to be addressed at the earliest opportunity. Despite the new Government's aversion to nuclear weapons, CPE found the newly installed ministers generally helpful and willing to assist. Notwithstanding this, the Polaris project remained a somewhat delicate subject with the Government, as Mackenzie was to discover. At the launching of HMS *Resolution* at Barrow in October 1967 the admiral was asked by a member of the press what he thought about the decision not to build the fifth submarine. Mackenzie was rather blunt and truthful in his reply; he was told to keep his mouth shut in future. On 8 December 1967, Frank Allaun, the MP for Salford East, asked the Secretary of State for Defence in the House of Commons whether Mackenzie's public speech was made with his authority, and if he would give an assurance that there not be an expansion of the Polaris programme. Healey replied that Mackenzie had not made a speech but had answered questions from the press at a briefing arranged by the shipbuilders. He added that decision not to proceed with the construction of a fifth Polaris submarine, of which he had informed the House on 15 February 1965, was unchanged.

Although there was still much work to be done, 1966 saw the first major milestones of the programme achieved. The Royal Navy Polaris School at Faslane was completed and formally opened on 30 June; at the end of the following month HMS *Valiant* was accepted into the Fleet; the first Polaris submarine, HMS *Resolution*, was launched on 15 September; and by the end of year the reactor test bed HMS *Warspite* had successfully completed her contractor's sea trials.

Meanwhile, Cammell Laird was falling behind schedule with its two submarines and there were still problems with procuring the steel for the hulls of the Fleet submarines. However, these problems were to fade into insignificance when hair-line cracks were found in the welds in the pressure hull of HMS *Dreadnought*. This had the potential to be disastrous and seriously disrupt the whole nuclear submarine building programme. A comprehensive ultrasonic survey of the affected welds was quickly implemented and fortunately showed that this was not a significant or generic problem.

During the year there were several changes in the management team. Admiral Mackenzie was more than aware that both naval personnel and civil servants normally changed post every two or three years and not to do so might affect their future careers. It says a lot about the admiral's generosity of spirit that he allowed his very successful team to be broken up to allow people to pursue their careers. Captain McKaig was relieved by Captain P. Higham as Deputy CPE; the Chief Administrative Officer, Bob Lewin, was replaced by Peter Nailor; and Captain La Niece was relieved by Captain C.H. Hammer in Washington. CPE made an exception to this with Charles Shepard, who was Head of the Polaris Weapon Section, and who, Mackenzie felt, was irreplaceable and should remain in post until the project was completed.

In the 1966 Defence Review the Wilson Government made significant cuts in the defence budget, and the review saw inter-service rivalries reach a new height. In the early 1960s the Navy had started planning the replacement for its aging aircraft carrier fleet, which was designated CVA-01. The RAF submitted a paper to the Treasury that compared the histories of carrier-borne and land-based bomber campaigns. Needless to say, the paper suggested that the new carriers and their supporting escort, the Type 82 destroyers, should be cancelled and the RAF could supply all the required support from land bases. There were also substantial reductions in the country's worldwide commitments but the Polaris project remained unaffected.

On 9 November 1967 Healey told the Commons: 'We have no intention of increasing the Polaris Force beyond its present planned strength of four submarines,' and on 6 December 1967, he emphasised that, 'the decision not to proceed with the construction at the fifth submarine … is unchanged'. On 14 February 1968 Healey said that he was quite satisfied that the Polaris submarines would provide an effective contribution to the Western nuclear strategic deterrent and reiterated, in answer to a supplementary question, that the contribution made by the four Polaris boats 'was a very substantial one indeed'.

During 1967 both HMS *Renown* and HMS *Repulse* were launched. Unfortunately, *Repulse* ran aground in the Walney Channel. Several CND anti-nuclear protesters had wedged themselves into the lock gates, delaying the launch by half an hour, which left insufficient clearance for *Repulse* to clear the mud. The launch was carried out by Lady Joan Zuckerman; wife of Sir Solly Zuckerman, Chief Scientific Advisor to the Government, who was also caught up in the CND demonstration. Despite this unfavourable start, *Repulse* went on to be the longest active survivor of the class; finally being decommissioned in 1996.

On 10 August 1967, the Clyde Submarine Base was officially commissioned (the formal opening was held on 10 May 1968 by HM Queen

Elizabeth, where it became officially known as the Clyde Submarine Base, HMS *Neptune*). HMS *Resolution* successfully completed contractor's sea trials and was accepted into service in October 1967. She then commenced a work-up period that culminated in her demonstration and shakedown operation (DASO), which involved the live firing of a missile in February 1968. Both HMS *Resolution* crews successfully completed DASO and the submarine was 'handed over' to her operating authority, C-in-C Home Fleet in June. Towards the end of the year it became apparent that the progress on the fourth submarine at Barrow, HMS *Repulse*, was so advanced that she would be completed before the third boat, HMS *Renown*, at Birkenhead. The programme was adjusted to take account of this. Also during 1967, as a consequence of the accidental flooding of SSBN02, the future HMS *Renown*, a further major readjustment of PMPs had to be undertaken in order to achieve recovery of the programme.

In August 1968 Admiral Mackenzie handed over to Rear Admiral A.F. Trewby, who became Assistant Controller (Polaris). He would ensure that the original build programme was completed and the submarines once in service had the necessary resources and facilities needed to keep them operational.

After an amazing five-and-a-half years of development, on 30 June 1969 the RAF formally handed over the responsibility for the nuclear deterrent to the Royal Navy.

In late 1973, Edward Heath's Conservative Government approved an upgrade to the Polaris missile. The early beginnings of studies to increase the likelihood of successful penetration of the Polaris warheads to Moscow began in 1964, even before the Polaris system was deployed, in order to preserve this capability in the face of anti-ballistic missile batteries around Moscow. This very secret project became known as 'Chevaline' and was the culmination of a year-long project that explored various possible solutions. These were to build more Polaris submarines; use a hardened missile, use a hardened missile with penetration aids, use an MIV warhead option, or – the Navy's preferred option – adopt the new American Poseidon missile, which had a greater range and carried more warheads than Polaris. Chevaline used a variety of penetration aids and decoys so that an enemy ABM system would be overwhelmed attempting to deal with them all, ensuring that enough warheads would get through and thereby guaranteeing an acceptable level of deterrence. This project remained secret through four different governments and was not disclosed until 24 January 1980 when Francis Pym, Secretary of State for Defence, speaking in a House of Commons debate on nuclear weapons, announced the existence of the Chevaline programme.

In 1982 Thatcher and Reagan reached an agreement to replace the British Polaris fleet with American-supplied Trident missiles. This was the culmination of a process started by the Callaghan Government a few years previously. It is interesting to note that during this period the same arguments that were raised during the Polaris project surfaced again, including how many boats would be required. David Owen, Defence Secretary in the Callaghan Government, wrote a paper that suggested, much to the horror of the Navy chiefs, that Fleet submarines could carry nuclear-armed cruise missiles, thereby doing away with the need for a dedicated missile submarine.

As the newer Vanguard-class submarines entered service, the Resolution-class vessels were gradually decommissioned. After 229 patrols, the Polaris fleet was finally decommissioned. HMS *Repulse* carried out the final Polaris patrol and was decommissioned at the End of Polaris Ceremony at Faslane on 28 August 1996. The Polaris Stone was dedicated and placed at the entrance to the Northern Area.

On 22 and 23 April 2013, a ceremony was held at Faslane to mark the fiftieth anniversary of the signing of the Polaris Agreement. During this ceremony, the Polaris Stone was moved to its new position in front of the Tyne Building and rededicated; perhaps to make room for a Trident Stone. Gerry McFeely's recalled the ceremony:

Having arrived in the Base in August '87, Resolution Class 'bombers' were a fairly common sight to me from that time through to the final decommissioning of HMS Repulse *in August '96. Whilst my main focus, by far, was the installation of Trident Vanguard as part of the Directorate of Naval Infrastructure & Environment (DNIE), which had emerged from Directorate of Quartering (Navy) subsequently to materialise as NBSA, and then reinvented as WSA; Reso Class was never far from my office window. Between the morning brief and the Wardroom back-bar scuttlebutt they kept me very much abreast of the 'ongoings' of our mutual affection and respect for the United Kingdom Independent Nuclear Deterrent. Reso with Polaris, if not a direct part of my desk work, was most definitely part of my life.*

I fully supported their move from the Southern Berths at 1 & 2, which had been their natural home for so many years, from 1968 I think, to 10, 11 & 12 Berths in the Northern Area. I believe I was instrumental in identifying and establishing the Squadron in Belmore House as the new Squadron HQ. The hardest part of that exercise was persuading Captain JWR (JOHN) Harris RN to leave the Command Building in Red Square and move north to Belmore House. John left the Base in late November 1996 and since he invited me to his RPC (leaving drinks) I must have been forgiven! This was just some four months after the end of Polaris with the decommissioning of HMS Repulse and the unveiling of the 'Polaris Monument' in the largely completed Northern Area of the Base.

Ten years after I retired, in April 2013 I was absolutely delighted to receive an invitation from the Squadron Cdr to attend the 50th Anniversary of the signing of Polaris Sales Agreement between the governments of the United States and our United Kingdom. I was honoured to accept as I saw it as a pleasant opportunity to catch up with some former colleagues, friends and RN stalwarts. The important event was scheduled to take place at Faslane (in the Supermess) over the Tues/Wed 22nd and 23rd April 2013. Transport was to be generously provided and Base access organised, but as I was an Hon Member of the Wardroom HMS Neptune, I did not need to avail myself of these essentials.

The two-day event was largely funded (95 per cent at least) and sponsored by the main and involved contractors over the last fifty years, with such illustrious names as AWE, Babcock, BAE Systems, Lockheed Martin, Mass, Qinetiq and Rolls-Royce. I understand that these industry partners were 'proud to support' the event. To balance the scales on that particular point I can state with some confidence that CSB/ HMNB Clyde Staff were equally proud to have programmed, maintained and managed the unbroken Deterrent Patrol, which had brought us to the present date. The Polaris Sales Agreement event was well organised throughout the two days and executed with military precision. The first evening, a superb buffet supper was provided in the Neptune Supermess from 1900–2200 and presented an ideal opportunity to seek out and catch up. In fact, for most of the guests the evening passed too quickly. Among the luminaries I met up with, bearing in mind I had been away for some ten years, included John Howie of Babcock, Ashley Lane of Mass, Cdr Don Milton of Coulport, Cdr J.H. Leatherby RN; Ron Laley and Ivor Jones, both of the Squadron, as well as Richard 'Taff' Evans [1st boat 1st patrol in Resolution] and many, many more of the 'Trade'. Cdr James 'Revenge' Richards RN was one of the many who could not appear due to operational commitments – a sense of duty!

We as Neptune Guests, all did our bit on the 'circulation front', ensuring none of the USN guests were abandoned and were completely at ease in the Neptune environment. Throughout the evening DVDs of the history of Polaris were viewed and 'thank you' speeches made with the evening concluding with the issue of com-memorative tokens (very posh!) being issued to all attendees.

The following day, under the guidance of Lt Cdr (later Cdr) Simon McCleary RN the plan was to marshal at the Chief's Mess and travel by Base Bus [310] along Maidstone Road to Belmore House for the rededication of the resited 'Polaris Monument'. The Service was conducted by the Rev Chaplain Richard Rowe with Cdre Steve Garrett Comfasflot escorting Rear Admiral Mark A. Beverstock Chief Strategic Systems Executive and his American counterpart T.J. Benedict USN Dir SSP. Several long retired Naval personnel including Cdre F.G. Thompson (with Dany) and COs both ashore and afloat also in attendance 'in full rig'.

If I have praised the organisers of the event highly enough and the buffet pro-viders likewise, my compliments must be recorded for the balanced and thoughtful Rededication Service. It included, along with Readings from Psalm 107 etc, the Polaris Prayer, the Naval Prayer and the Prayer for World Peace, concluding with the Benediction and the joint unveiling of the Polaris Monument by CSSE & Dir SSP.

A moving 'moment of silence' finalised the ceremony and all moved off to admire the 'stone', say fond farewells and leave to meet their transport arrangements for the journey home. For my own part I was honoured to be present on such an important occasion in the history of the Base – proud to be part of it, a lifelong memory.

4

AND SO TO WORK

When the submarines were launched, they joined the newly formed 10th Submarine Squadron at Faslane. The Squadron was originally established at Devonport on 10 December 1914 on the depot ship HMS *Forth*. The flotilla was disbanded on 2 March 1919, then reformed on 1 September 1941 at Malta, with the submarines being based at HMS *Talbot* on Manoel Island in Marsamxett Harbour. The small U-class submarines of the 'Fighting 10th' severely disrupted enemy supply lines to Northern Africa, sinking or damaging 1,056,000 tons of shipping. The flotilla was disbanded on 21 September 1944.

The squadron was re-formed at Faslane on 1 February 1967 and would eventually consist of the four newly built Polaris submarines. Between 15 June 1968 and 15 May 1996, the four submarines carried out a total of 229 operational patrols, ensuring the British nuclear, Continuous At Sea Deterrent (CASD), was ready at all times.

10th Submarine Squadron (SM 10) (Feb 1967–Sep 1993)

Captain SM10

Captain K. Vause
The Lord Fieldhouse of Gosport GCB GBE
Admiral Sir Peter Herbert KCB OBE
Captain M.C. Henry
Captain J.R. Wadman OBE
Captain R.G. Fry OBE
Captain A.E. Thomson CBE
Captain C. Grant
Captain F.D. Lowe
Captain R.H. Farnfield
Commodore T.D. Elliot
Commodore A.M. Gregory OBE
Captain R.J. Bradshaw

On 1 October 1993, the 3rd and 10th Submarine Squadrons combined to emerge as the 1st Submarine Squadron (SM1). The new Captain SM1 was Captain McLees, who was previously Captain SM3.

1st Submarine Squadron (SM 1) (1 Oct 1993–)

Captain SM1

Captain J. McLees
Captain J.W.R. Harris

(Images: User: Legohead – Own work, Public Domain.)

The Submarines

All four submarines were essentially the same apart from minor cosmetic differences, although as mentioned in Chapter 3, HMS *Renown* was 1in longer than her sister submarines.

General specifications for the submarines were:

Displacement, surfaced	7,500–7,600 tons
Displacement, submerged	8,400–8,500 tons
Length, O/A	425ft (129.5m)–426ft (130m)
Max Beam	33ft (10.1m)
Draft	30ft 1in (9.2m)
Propulsion	Nuclear reactor PWR.1 pressurised water
Engines	Steam turbines
Number of main engines	2
Main engine builder	English Electric Steam Turbines
Main power	27,500shp (20,500kW)
Propeller(s)	1
Speed, surface	20 knots (37km/h)
Speed, submerged	24 knots (44km/h)
Diving depth	In excess of 1,000ft
Endurance	Unlimited except by food supplies
Electronics	Ferranti DCB fire control system
Weapons Systems	Sixteen tubes for Polaris, six torpedo tubes for Tigerfish or Spearfish torpedoes, Royal Navy Sub-Harpoon (RNSH) anti-ship missiles
Complement	143–156

HMS Resolution (SS22/SSBN01)

'Resolute and Vigilant'

Laid down: 28 Feb 1964
Launched: 15 Sept 1966 (Vickers Ltd, Barrow-in-Furness) by
HM Queen Elizabeth, The Queen Mother
Commissioned: 2 Oct 1967
Decommissioned: 22 Oct 1994
Patrols: 61

Fired the first British submarine Polaris missile on 15 February 1968 whilst on demonstration and shakedown operations (DASO) off Cape Kennedy, Florida.

Commanding Officers

Captain M.C. Henry ADC
Commander K.D. Frewer OBE
Commander R.H. Mann
Commodore G.A.S. Paul ADC
Captain N.A.D. Grant
Commander U. Hoggarth
Captain A.E. Thomson CBE
Captain H. Peltor CBE
Commodore I.D.C. Ross
Captain R.M. Venables
Commodore C.J. Meyer OBE
Commodore T.D. Elliott

Commodore P. Branscombe OBE
Commander M.J. Sime
Commander N.J.K. Crews
Commodore A.M. Gregory OBE
Captain H. Keay
Commander P.J. Christmas
Commander J.R.C. Foster
Captain A.M. Poulter OBE
Captain D.M. Tall OBE
Commander M.B. Avery
Captain P.J. Walker
Commander J. Powis

HMS Renown (SS26/SSBN02)

'Guardian of an ancient renown'

Laid down: 26 Jun 1964
Launched: 25 Feb 1967 (Cammell Laird, Merseyside) by Mrs Healey
Commissioned: 15 Nov 1968
Decommissioned: 1996
Patrols   52

Commanding Officers

Captain R.J.P. Heath CBE
Captain K.H. Mills
Commander A.G.A. Pogson
Commander H.N.M. Thompson
Commander F.N. Ponsonby LVO
  OBE
Commander K.R.B. Cadogan-
  Rawlinson OBE
Commodore M.H. Everett
Rear Admiral J.S. Lang
Commander R.C. Whiteside OBE
Commander J.N. Franklin

Commodore D.M. Jefferys ADC
Commander D.M. O'Brien
Commander D.L.P. Evans
Commodore A.M. Gregory OBE
Commander M.G. Jones
Captain R.F. Strange
Commander R.J.K. Burston
Commander D.S. Morris
Commander G. Webster
Commander T.R. Herman
Commander I.D. Arthur

HMS Repulse (SS23/SSBN03)

'Who touches me is broken'

Laid down: Mar 1965
Launched: 4 Nov 1967 (Vickers Ltd, Barrow-in-Furness)
                        by Lady Zuckerman
Commissioned: 28 Sept 1968
Decommissioned: 28 Aug 1996
Patrols: 60

The second Polaris submarine to enter service. During her first commission she completed eight deterrent patrols.

Commanding Officers

Commander J.R. Wadman OBE   Commander J.N. Ferguson
Commander R.C. Seaward   Captain T.D.A. Thompson CBE
Rear Admiral A.J. Whetstone CB   Commander A.J.K. Nicoll
Commander R.L.P. Jones MBE   Commander D.M. O'Brien
Commander C.A.W. Russell OBE   Commander C.D.I. Stockman
Commander J.H. Gordon   Commander W.M. Logan
Commander A.D.C. Lund OBE   Commander I.S.H. Richards
Captain J.L. Milnes   Commodore P.L. Bryan
Commander T.H. Green OBE   Commander G. Webster
Captain D.J. Russell   Commodore C.W. Roddis
Commander J.N. Colquhoun   Commander D.G. Phillips
Commander J.J. Tall OBE   Captain R.J. Bradshaw
Commander N.B. Shacklock

HMS Revenge (SS27/SSBN04)

'Shine with untarnished honour'

Laid down: May 1964
Launched: 15 Mar 1968 (Cammell Laird Merseyside) by Lady Law
Commissioned: 4 Dec 1968
Decommissioned: May 1992
Patrols: 56

Commanding Officers

Commander W.I. Morrison | Commander S.J. Hayward
Commander B.R. Coward OBE | Rear Admiral A.P. Hoddinott
Captain J.B.L. Watson | Commander P.J. Christmas
Commander V. McVittie | Commander A.M. Bruce
Captain F.D. Lowe | Commander R.C. Seaward
Captain R.S. Wraith | Vice Admiral Sir Toby Frere KCB
Captain M.E. Ortmans LVO | Commander M. Avery
Captain J.L. Milne | Commander H.K.P. Michell
Captain G. Jaques | Commander D.S. Morris
Commander A.F.M. Taylor | Captain R.M. Gee
Captain A.M.D. Milne-Holme CB
   OBE

The fifth submarine would have been called HMS *Ramillie*. It was cancelled in 1965.

The torpedo compartment on HMS *Revenge*.
(Open Government Licence v3.0)

COMMISSIONED
4th December 1969
CAMMELL LAIRDS, BIRKENHEAD

RECOMMISSIONED
19th April 1975
HM Naval Base, ROSYTH

**HMS REVENGE
RECOMMISSION**
4th SEPTEMBER, 1982
HM NAVAL BASE, ROSYTH

HMS *Revenge* recommissioning booklet.

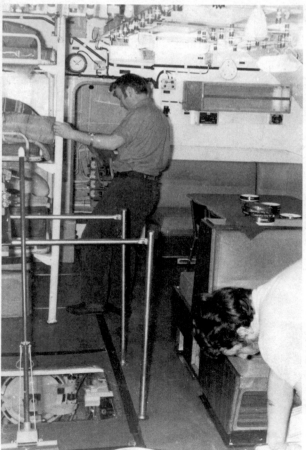

Above: Junior rates dining hall on HMS *Revenge*, (Open Government Licence v3.0)

Left: Junior rates recreational space (upper level torpedo compartment) on HMS *Revenge*.

HMS *Resolution*'s first commanding officers: Commanders M.C. Henry (left) and K.D. Frewer (right).

HMS *Revenge* (P) 199. Members of the senior rates mess handing over a cheque to Erskine Hospital. The money was raised by the mess during the patrol.

Ex-HMS *Repulse* commanding officers at the 'Goodbye Repulse Dinner' c. 1992. From left to right: Cdr Bob Seaward, Cdr Barry Coward, Cdr Ian Morrison, Cdr Tony Taylor, Capt Frank Lowe, Cdr Peter Christmas, Cdre (now) Malcolm Avery, Capt Mike Farr, Cdr Robin Gee, Rear Admiral Toby Frere, Capt Basil Watson. Standing: Capt John Milnes, Cdr David Morris.

Ex COs arriving for the dinner.

One-man control. (Open Government Licence v3.0)

Christmas at sea on HMS *Repulse*.

Above: After an unfortunate incident with the sewage tank, HMS *Resolution*'s first lieutenant, Lt Cdr Seaward, said that AMS 1 should be cleaned so he could eat his dinner 'down there'. The boys did a very good job, so good in fact that the first lieutenant had to eat his own words.

Left: ...and the first lieutenant tucks in.

USN *Observation Island*.

The ship's company on casing. HMS *Repulse*. (Open Government Licence v3.0)

Left: HMS *Resolution*'s commissioning. (Open Government Licence v3.0)

Below: HMS *Resolution*'s first DASO in the USA. (Open Government Licence v3.0)

The wardroom on
HMS *Repulse*. (Open
Government Licence v3.0)

HMS *Resolution*'s first
DASO programme.

The wardroom on
HMS *Repulse*. (Open
Government Licence v3.0)

Left: What it was all about.

Below: The four Polaris submarines tied up at Rosyth dockyard await final disposal, perhaps not quite a fitting end.

Renown and Repulse

Resolution and Revenge

Churchill, Dreadnought and Swiftsure

Left: Horse racing night.

Below: Cdr Seaward, CO HMS *Repulse*, used to complain that, while he spent a great deal of time handing out medals at his table, he never got one, so his senior rates made him an LSGC, bless 'em.

Families Day: Mrs V. Dance tries her hand at driving the submarine.

The boat transfer at Loch Long for Families Day.

From the end of the Second World War until the 1970s the Submarine Service was effectively 'all volunteer', with approximately 450 men volunteering a year. While this was more than enough to meet the manpower requirements of the conventional flotilla, to man the rapidly growing nuclear submarine fleet compulsory drafting was introduced and personnel were drawn from all branches of the Navy. I can remember a Fleet Air Arm engineer who became a Nuclear Chief of the Watch, and amongst the fledgling Health Physics branch were writers, stokers and meteorologists, apart from the source branch medical branch ratings. The first five health physics ratings trained in America along with many other nuclear or missile personnel. Some even served on American submarines.

In the case of personnel destined for the Polaris programme, their new home was to be the largest submarines ever built for the Royal Navy, complete with facilities undreamed of in the conventional diesel submarine fleet. Even the new nuclear fleet submarines could not match the accommodation to be found on the Polaris submarines.

Regardless of the crew's origins, this 400ft, three-decked steel tube would be their home for the three-month on-crew period. On boarding, you enter the submarine via the main access hatch, and the ladder descends to one deck. Forward is the sonar console space, which housed the electrical equipment, associated with the submarine's sonar. To the left is the sonar office, where crew members operated the sonar sets and their associate displays. On the right-hand side (starboard) is the wireless office; a very important space as the submarine had to stay in communication or be able to receive messages from the control authority at all times while on patrol. Aft of this is the control room, from where the submarine was operated. On the forward bulkhead is the one-man control, although normally operated by two men. Similar to an aircraft joystick, the stick to the right controls rudder and foreplanes, while the one on the left operates the aft planes that control the depth and angle of the submarine in the water. The operators of these controls were known as the 'planesmen'.

Behind the planesmen sat the Ship Control Officer of the Watch (SCOOW), who was responsible for general ships safety. He controlled the trim of the submarine and initiated any remedial actions to emergency situations.

Just behind and to the left of the SCOOW is the systems console; this panel controls the ship's hydraulic and high-pressure air systems. It also controls the submarine's buoyancy; six main ballast tanks and several auxiliary or trim tanks can be alternately filled with water or air. On the surface, the ballast tanks are filled with air. As the submarine dives, air is vented from the ballast tanks, they are flooded with water and the submarine begins to sink. To surface the submarine, high pressure air is blown into the tanks, forcing the water out. The compressed air is stowed in a series of bottle groups, large cylinders. In an emergency that requires the submarine to surface quickly, a system called emergency blow fills the ballast tanks rapidly with high-pressure air.

The chart table is on the right-hand side of the control room. This is not normally used once the submarine is on patrol when navigation is coordinated by the navigation centre, situated at the back of the control room. Once on patrol it was essential that the Polaris weapon system knew the exact position of the submarine prior to missile launch. Initially this information was supplied by Loran-C, which relied on fixed shore-based radio beacons. Eventually this system was replaced by the Ships Inertial Navigation System (SINS). This used a computer that processed data from motion sensors (accelerometers) and rotation sensors (gyroscopes) to continuously calculate the position of the submarine. At the back of the control room, on the right-hand side, is a ladder to two deck.

Descending the forward ladder to two deck, the garbage eject space is to the left; initially the domestic-generated waste was compacted and 'ejected' from the submarine via a 'vertical' torpedo tube, the 'gash gun'. Nowadays, to comply with international laws, all rubbish is stored on the submarine until it returns to port. The galley is directly in front of you. In this small compartment the three chefs provided breakfast, a two-course lunch and a three-course dinner for approximately 150 people. There was also a 'middle watch' breakfast at 0400 for off-going watch keepers. During an eight-week patrol, the chefs would prepare more than 33,000 meals; the equivalent of feeding a family of four for five years.

Looking forward, on the right-hand side of the galley is the junior rates dining room, while forward of the galley on the port side is the scullery, where the infamous 'Peter the Eater', the garbage grinder, lived.

• •

In the days of Mick-the-Munch, or Peter the Eater, when we ditched our gash [rubbish] at sea, a young part 3 RO [trainee radio operator] had stowed his civvies in a poly [plastic] bag, this was then stowed in a normal gash bag. However, he was called to an exercise fire in the Radar Shack. Following the exercise his gash bag was rounded up with the rest of the day's rubbish and guess what, yessss it went into Mick the Munch. A lesson well learnt for a Pt 3.

Tony Smyth

• •

Just forward of the scullery was the ship's canteen; a small shop that sold an amazing array of sweets, soft drinks and assorted trinkets. Forward of this through the watertight hatch in 35 bulkhead is the torpedo compartment, the upper level is used as the junior rates recreation space. This level also houses the ship's library, a couple of stowage compartments and the anchor control compartment, and this area is often used as an 'overspill' bunk space. The compartment also doubled as an escape compartment (the forward escape compartment). On the lower level is the actual torpedo compartment.

Returning to the junior rates dining hall, looking aft and on the right side is the senior rates mess, which was originally used as a senior rates lounge and dining room. This compartment also doubled as an emergency operating theatre.

•••

I remember to prepare the Senior Rates Mess as an emergency operating theatre. We had to cover the bulkheads in polythene, there was a fitting in the deckhead for an operating lamp and screw holes in the deck for the portable operating table. This was all in the after part of the mess, near the bar; I'm not sure of the significance of that.

Author

•••

Opposite and just aft of the garbage eject space is a small store and bunk space; this was converted to the, much appreciated, senior rates dining room during all the Polaris submarines first refits. Aft of this was the upper senior rates bunk space. Aft of this, all the way to the forward missile compartment bulkhead is the wardroom. On the starboard side, aft of the senior rates mess, is a small sick bay, then the ship's office, where the leading writer kept the submarine's administration organised and up to date. Next is the coxswain's office, then the air conditioning space and the aft ladder to the control room.

Three deck houses the junior rates main sleeping accommodation, and bathroom and heads the ship's laundry, senior rates bunk space and bathroom and heads. Auxiliary Machinery Space (AMS) 1 (is accessed from three deck. This compartment houses a hydraulic plant, bilge and ballast pumps. Aft on three deck is the missile control centre, which houses the computers and equipment required to target and launch the missiles. Under three deck are a variety of water tanks and the main battery.

The aft ladder from three deck leads to two deck, just forward of the hatch into the missile compartment. This large three-decked compartment contains the sixteen missile tubes; 8ft in diameter and 30ft tall. It is often referred to as 'Sherwood Forrest' in books but I must admit I've never heard this term used on board a British Polaris submarine. This compartment houses the IMP, which monitors the missile tube environment and on the port side on two deck, the health physics laboratory.

The HP lab doubled as a dark room, so the medics were often the ship's photographers. The fact that the lab was a dark room came from the early days of the programme, when the crew wore film badges to measure the amount of radiation they received. These badges were developed by the medics in the lab. (In the late 1960s the dosimetry service was centralised at the Institute of Naval Medicine at Alverstoke in the Admiralty Radiation Record Centre, ARRC)

Author

The Polaris office and the tech office are also on the middle level of the missile compartment, along with the stores department, who had a small office and stowage racks on this level. The submarines carried several thousand stores items enabling the crew to repair emergent defects without breaking the patrol.

The next compartment is AMS 2. This was the compartment proposed by Mr Palmer to overcome the problems in joining an American MC on to a British stern section. On one deck are some of the ship's atmosphere purification equipment, including three carbon dioxide scrubbers, which removed carbon dioxide, an unwanted product of respiration from the submarine's atmosphere, and discharged it overboard. Opposite these were two electrolysers, which supplied the oxygen the crew required. There was also a CO/H2 burner that removed carbon monoxide and hydrogen from the atmosphere. On two deck were the Freon removal plants and on three deck were the two diesel generators.

Aft of AMS 2 is the reactor compartment. The nuclear reactor supplies the hot water that produces the steam that powers the submarine's propulsion turbines and electrical generators. Across the top of this compartment is a passageway known as the Tunnel; this provides access, the only access, from forward to aft of the submarine.

Aft of the reactor compartment is AMS 3. On one deck is the manoeuvring room, a compartment jam-packed with electrical cabinets from where the reactor, electrical production and the speed of the submarine is controlled. On two deck there is more control equipment for reactor control and two motor generators. On three deck are two turbo generators that supply the ship's electrical needs when the reactor is critical. Aft of this is the engine room, which houses the main turbines that drive the submarine. The final compartment is the motor room, which houses the submarine's electrical propulsion motor and doubles as an escape compartment, a very cramped escape compartment.

This very brief tour gives very little indication of the vast amount of other equipment, lockers, pipes, electrical cabling and firefighting equipment that are, seemingly, crammed into any available space on board the submarine. It was rumoured that during the build the first 'docky' down the boat was the one who got his pipe in straight; everybody else, after him, had to bend their pipes around his.

During the early stages of the programme, Jimmy Launders, a submarine commander on the project team, produced a series of operational deployment plans for the Polaris force; depending on whether there would be four or five submarines. He based his plans on the American system where each submarine had two crews; although the British opted for the traditional Port and Starboard, not Blue and Gold as used by the US Navy. The cycle was based on a fifty-six-day patrol and a twenty-eight-day maintenance and turnaround period; estimates for refit/refuelling periods were gleaned from the somewhat limited information from the Dreadnought programme. All this information was transferred to a very impressive bar chart that was initially used to try and convince the Government that five submarines would be required to guarantee a minimal deterrent; two boats on patrol to allow for one aborting unexpectedly. This also formed the basic patrol pattern in the early years of the programme and it was not unusual for members of the crews to be able to book holidays two years in advance, safe in the knowledge that they would be available on the pre-booked date. Even before the first refits it was becoming apparent that the programme would 'slip'. As the submarines aged the cycles became increasingly unpredictable and occasionally the dreaded 'Repent' signal was sent. This meant that there was some problem with the submarine due to go on patrol and the on-patrol submarine was required to stay at sea. The longest patrol was completed by HMS *Resolution* in 1991, which lasted 108 days. Normally when a Polaris submarine returns from sea, the stores organisation sends chacons (cargo containers) to the jetty, so the crew can offload the remaining food. When HMS *Resolution* came alongside, the PO chef could carry the remaining food off in a (not very full) black gash sack.

••

During the Reso long patrol I remember the Skipper calling his HODs (Heads of Department) and Departmental Chiefs to a meeting where he asked them to compile lists of stores they would require to keep the boat at sea if the next boat due on patrol couldn't sail. If necessary it was planned to restore the submarine at sea. A senior rate asked, 'Do you think if we asked for more missiles they'd bring us home?'

Author

••

Intensive inspection routines and complicated repairs further impacted the patrol cycles, resulting in periods of two-boat Continuous at Sea Deterrent. These periods of one boat at sea and one in maintenance were, at best, demanding for the crews and the inboard support staff. These were also very trying times for the families.

Within the cycle, during the off-crew crews would be granted leave, many would take professional courses and there were endless courses or training sessions that enabled the crew to stay qualified for their on-board watch-keeping positions. Planesmen, system console watch keepers and ship control officers of the watch trained in a simulated control room that was similar to the aircraft simulators used to train pilots. Manoeuvring room watch keepers were trained in a replica manoeuvring room, called 'NuScot', where various computer-generated incidents could be simulated. Sonar watch keepers had a similar facility and Polaris personnel used the Polaris School. There were many organised off-crew activities; tank driving, I remember, was very popular for a period, parachuting, sailing and taking the squadron MFV out for a cruise around the local lochs. For the married members of the crew it was a period to catch up with family life.

Once a crew went on-crew there were normally two days of work up (harbour training) to ensure the men were competent to man the submarine and deal with any potential incidents; fire, missile emergencies, etc., and to re-familiarise themselves with on-board routines. The two crews of the first submarine, HMS *Resolution*, did not really get on well together. The commanding officers of the later submarines tried to avoid this division; sports days were not held between the two crews but between combined departments. In the early days the two crews did not really work closely together, things were often stowed in different locations, even different drawers; paperwork for the same task was often different and a great deal of time was spent changing things to the on-crew way. Luckily this attitude moderated over the years with the two crews working more closely together.

A few days after going on-crew the maintenance period started; an intensive maintenance and repair period that included planned routine maintenance and any emergent work that became apparent while the submarine was at sea. These periods became increasingly demanding as the submarines aged. The submarines were subject to an annual 'programmed' docking between refits. Occasionally, operational requirements led to the vessels being docked at short notice. Originally, this maintenance period was programmed to last seventeen days, as mentioned – seventeen very busy days. At the end of this, the submarine sailed on a short work-up period. Sometimes the submarines carried out trials. After this, the submarine returned to the armaments depot at Coulport to load missiles and torpedoes. After a few days, the submarine would sail on patrol, and often some of the crew's wives would drive their cars down the loch side road, 'accompanying' the submarine as she sailed on patrol. Initially these patrols were eight weeks long, but this again slipped as the submarines got older.

Another feature of the maintenance period was the possibility of the Nuclear Weapons Inspection (NWI) or the even worse the Snap NWI, where the inspection team would turn up unannounced and subject the crew to a thorough examination on all aspects of nuclear weapon security and safety and conduct a series of exercises and drills to show the crew were able to deal with all nuclear weapon emergencies. Certain members of the crew were subjected to in depth interviews to ensure they had the required depth of knowledge. A number of lectures and exercises were conducted throughout the maintenance period to make sure the crew had the necessary information.

On completion of the maintenance period, the submarine would sail on work-up; several days, sometimes weeks, of extensive exercises designed to ensure the crew could cope with any accident or emergency that might befall them.

∙∙

After numerous false alarms from the after A.P.D. (Air Particle Detector), the maintainer made this report to the D.M.E.O. [Deputy Marine Engineering Officer] in the Manoeuvring Room:

> *Chief Mech, 'This A.P.D. is in the wrong place Sir.'*
> *D.M.E.O. 'Wrong place Chief, and where should it be?'*
> *Chief Mech, 'on the f*****g Valiant Sir.'*

Tony Smyth

∙∙

When the submarine sailed on patrol, the majority of the crew fell into a watch system. Normally this was one in three (four hours on, eight hours off). While the engineers remained in this watch-keeping system over the years, other departments adopted different systems, and some even worked 'days'. To assess the effects of the various watch-keeping systems on the crews over such a prolonged period, HMS *Renown* took a physiatrist on patrol, enabling him to evaluate the crew's performance. Several members of the crew, representing the various watch-keeping systems, were selected to undergo psychometric tests three times a day and a blood sample was taken daily. The physiatrist also carried out regular interviews with crew members. The submarines' medical officers were often given 'patrol projects'. The aim of these was to assess the effects of being in an enclosed environment for prolonged periods. In the early days it was rumoured that this research would be used to assess the effects of long durations of separation on space crews, although I think this might have been just a little fanciful thinking.

During the off-watch time the crew had to eat, sleep and relax. Food became extraordinarily important and was of vital importance in influencing crew morale. The food had a secondary, but nevertheless important, function; as time morphed into an endless series of watches, it acted as a sort of culinary calendar. There were 'seggies' (grapefruit slices) for breakfast on Sunday, fish on Fridays, steak night on Saturday, a big Sunday roast. The chefs also prepared mess dinners. These traditional, very formal, meals would be held once a patrol: in the case of the junior and senior rates, each mess would 'serve the other'.

To occupy the rest of the off-watch time there were many activities. The submarines had a library and crew members brought their own books, which were often traded once read. Films were very popular; initially the infamous Bell and Howell 35mm, which was augmented by videos and DVDs as these became more popular and available in civilian life.

When he wasn't involved with his medical trials, the medical officer organised many of the off-watch activities. Quizzes, of various sorts, were very popular and keenly fought.

••

Reso dit: We had a quiz night on a Saturday. It was done like University Challenge. You had to give your name, college and subjects studied.

It went something like this:

First Lt: Granger, Jesus College, Cambridge, reading physics, chemistry and maths.
POMA [Petty Officer Medical Assistant]: Smyth, Balliol College, Oxford,
reading gas meters and Noggin the Nog.
First Lt: You are not taking this seriously.

Tony Smyth

••

There were also an assortment of games nights, often played between the
three messes (wardroom, senior rates and junior rates). These ranged from
cards, dominoes and darts with chess and bridge for the clever ones. Horse
racing nights were popular, where home-made horses powered by the roll of
a dice would race round the junior rates dining hall. During off-watch periods, individual mess members often passed the time by playing crib, where
the mess would reverberate to shouts of 'you timber-shifting b★★★★★d' or 'fifteen two that b★★★★★d'. In an attempt to restore the peace in the mess there
was the ever-popular Uckers; a grown-up's version of Ludo. Played by two or
four players, the rules would take a lifetime to learn. It is said that if MENSA
members played a board game, then that board game would be Uckers.

Pub nights were popular, these allowed the crew to demonstrate their
karaoke skills, or not as the case may be. All the submarines produced a 'ship's
magazine', essentially a local newspaper that operated on the old journalistic
principle of never letting the truth get in the way of a good story. During
the patrol, there would be a sods opera, an even more politically incorrect
variety-type show. HMS *Renown*, during the first commission, celebrated
'Mid Patrol Day' with a 'village fair', with crew members running stalls to
raise money for charity. The patrol length was a little more predictable in the
early days of the programme. Some crews produced radio programmes that
were 'broadcast' over the ship's tannoy system,

Many of the crew had hobbies; painting was popular but restrictions on
what chemicals could be taken to sea because of possible atmospheric con-
taminants were an important consideration. That aside, some people made
fishing rods, I remember someone fly-tying; others did calligraphy, wood-
work, military modelling, and even knitting. The back afties, with access to
lathes, drills, etc., produced all sorts of amazing things. Generally, the quality
of work produced on board was astonishingly good. HMS *Resolution* at one
stage used to have an arts and crafts competition that culminated in a 'show'
at the end of patrol; the junior rates dining hall was used as a show room.
Some submarines had pop groups, some even had a brass band.

Many members of the crew used off-watch time to pursue further education, taking the opportunity to increase NAMET grades, a naval exam in maths and English. Certain ranks required a certain NAMET score. Others did GCEs, some studied for higher rate exams, while others did Open University courses. All this was the remit of the medical officer, who, amongst his many responsibilities, was the education officer. During the early years of the programme three crew members studied for their private pilot's licence while on patrol; one even went on to become a commercial airline pilot after he left the Navy.

The submarines carried a variety of keep fit equipment, often in the missile compartment, and these comprised weights, rowing machines, and exercise bikes. Some submarines even organised exercise classes in the junior rates dining hall. The submarines raised large amounts of money for charity; crew members from HMS *Resolution* 'cycled' round the world' on the boat's exercise bike during one patrol, raising funds to buy special beds for a local old people's home.

Another popular pursuit in the early days of the programme was, believe it or not, wine making. Often Rise 'n' Shine, the powdered breakfast drink, was used as a base, although I remember a very cheeky teabag wine from the sunny slopes of AMS 2 during HMS *Renown*'s first commission. We medics, pessimistic to the end, would wring our hands in fear, prophesising the dire effects the fermenting wine would have on the ship's atmosphere. These doom-laden forecasts did not seem to be supported by routine atmosphere monitoring.

Once the submarine sailed, the crews were allowed duty free privileges; tobacco, drink and even perfume. When not at sea, smokers were entitled to Navy cigarettes, fondly referred to as 'Pussers Blue Liners'. They were issued to naval personnel at shore bases or to ships alongside. Every month each eligible person would receive three cigarette coupons, each coupon entitling the holder to 100 cigarettes or a tin of tobacco.

There are some that would say the sole purpose of the Polaris submarine was to transport senior rates' beer around the world, although with the small numbers that used to appear at 'load beer', it's hard to believe that many mess members actually drank. One of the more creative ways of storing beer was to use the barrels as seats. Until 31 July 1970 (Black Tot Day, when the tot was stopped) submariners, along with the rest of the Royal Navy, were issued a daily rum ration. Normally the tot was issued at lunchtime, although those going on watch drew their tot later. Tot time was a great social occasion, favours were paid for with sippers or gulpers, where shipmates were allowed a small sip or larger sip, depending on the nature of the favour.

The submariners received a short daily news sheet that was passed round the messes. The crews also received weekly 'family grams', these were twenty-word (forty words once a month) messages from the next of kin, and were a very important factor in crew morale.

Interdenominational church services were held each Sunday morning while the submarine was at sea, and these were, generally, well attended. The musical backing for the hymns was provided by a small treadle-powered organ. To make things a little easier for the organist, some submarines used a vacuum cleaner to provide the air to power the organ.

* * *

I remember an incident, 1st commish, Reso, [first time in service] 2/3 rd trip, port. On a Sunday, a church service was held in the Sr rates dining hall, the organ was powered by the outlet of a cylinder hoover. Bungy and me were messmen [on duty tidying the mess] that trip, after setting up the said organ a certain person decided it would be a good idea to fill the bag with foofoo [talcum] powder. All were assembled for the singsong, as soon as the keys were pushed the complete contents of the hoover bag exited through the organ, covering all and sundry in a dusting of white powder, the ensuing exit from the service was amusing. Now not only did the bun house have a total sense of humour failure, us two messmen got a bollocking for said prank. Appy Daze.

On Renown, just after commissioning, the fwd staff thought that using a noisy vacuum cleaner to power the ship's organ spoiled the service, so they decided to connect the organ to the EBS (Emergency Breathing System). Come Sunday, when it was time for the first hymn, a fwd stoker proudly opened the valve on the temporary air supply line, the organist pressed the keys for the opening cord. There was a strange wheezing sound, which was followed by a very loud bang as the organ exploded.

'Arry Arnott

* * *

It was customary for a VIP to meet the returning submarine; this was probably a carryover from the US Navy, where the returning SSBN would be met by a senior naval officer. In Britain, the Control Authority kept a list of prominent politicians and senior military officers who would be asked to visit the incoming submarine. From the first patrol, the crew's next of kin were invited to Coulport to meet the submarine returning from patrol. This eventually was discontinued; understandably, after several long weeks at sea, the crew just wanted to finish the work and get home.

Preventative medicine played a large part in ensuring that the submarines could meet their deployment dates; during the first few years of the programme all crews had yearly flu shots. In the early days, along with the VIP, staff from the dental department also joined the submarine, the idea being that they could examine the whole crew before they disappeared on weekend leave or the distractions of off-crew life made attendance at the dental clinic a particularly unattractive option.

Initially the general public were very interested in these new submarines. In response to this, in the early 1970s, Yorkshire Television made a documentary about life on board a Polaris submarine. They filmed HMS *Renown*'s Starboard crew berthing at Coulport on return from patrol; as was custom in the early days of the programme, the next of kin were waiting on the jetty. The ship's brass band was on the casting playing 'Hearts of Oak', the only tune they could play. Unfortunately, the throttles jammed open and the boat just steamed passed the jetty. In the finest traditions of the service, the band kept playing until the submarine finally came alongside. John Winton's 1971 book *The Fighting Temeraire* features a fictional British Polaris submarine HMS *Temeraire*, which is used on a spying mission in the Black Sea. The author went to sea on HMS *Renown* for a pre-patrol work-up period to research the book.

All this aside, the submarine was a weapon system and its main purpose was, once on patrol, to remain undetected and to be ready to launch its missiles at fifteen minutes' notice whenever required

Only the Prime Minister or an approved deputy could authorise a nuclear launch. There was a closed-circuit television system link between 10 Downing Street and the Polaris control officer at Northwood. Both the Prime Minister and the control officer were able to see each other on their monitors when the command was given. If the link failed, for example during a nuclear attack or when the Prime Minister was away from Downing Street, he would send an authentication code that could be verified at Northwood. The Commander-in-Chief would then broadcast a firing order to the Polaris submarines via the very low frequency radio station at Rugby. Britain did not use a system requiring codes to be sent before weapons can be launched, such as the American Permissive Action Link. It is perhaps the first safety interlock in the system, it is not the Prime Minister who actually tells the submarine captain to launch his missiles, it is the Commander-in-Chief.

If for some reason the Prime Minister was unable to authorise the launch, each captain of a Polaris submarine had a handwritten letter from him or her, which contained instructions on what action he should take in the event that Britain was obliterated by nuclear attack and all those who had authority to authorise the launch were dead. This was pertinently known as 'The Letter of Last Resort'. How the submarine's captain would actually determine if Britain was under attack included whether or not BBC Radio 4 continued broadcasting. The on-patrol submarine was reported to have briefly gone on nuclear alert in 2004 when Radio 4 mysteriously went off the air for fifteen minutes.

Once the signal was received on board, the submarine would be brought to 'action stations missile', the signal would be authenticated by two officers and the missiles would be prepared to be launched within fifteen minutes. There were a number of safety interlocks normally requiring activation by a series of special keys. While on patrol the submarines regularly practised the missile launch procedure, this was the Weapon System Readiness Test (WSRT).

It was reported by the *New Statesman* during the Falklands War that the Government had ordered the on-patrol Polaris submarine, HMS *Resolution*, to move to the south and patrol off Ascension Island, giving the British Government the option of a nuclear strike against Argentina if the Royal Navy lost a capital ship. The ship's company were very surprised to hear this on the BBC's World News, Commander Elliot, HMS *Resolution*'s commanding officer, ridiculed the report on his return to Faslane. As a strange aside to this, later in the year Ali Magoudi, Francois Mitterrand's psychiatrist, published his diary, in which he mentioned that the French Prime Minister had arrived late for a meeting on 7 May 1982, several days after HMS *Sheffield* was sunk in an Exocet attack. He allegedly told Magoudi that the delay was due to a telephone call from a very irate Margaret Thatcher, demanding the codes that would 'inactivate' the Exocet missiles; she promised nuclear strikes against Argentina if the codes were not released.

EPILOGUE

By any measure, the British Polaris project was a colossal undertaking; each of its constituent parts was a massive venture in its own right and considering the fact they were all completed, simultaneously, on time and to budget, that undoubtedly makes this project a unique and remarkable achievement. It was a fact that was recognised by the Chairman of the Public Accounts Committee, who suggested in the early 1970s that the Polaris programme could 'act as an example of an effective, well-managed project that should be used as a model for future Government projects'. Unfortunately, his advice was thoroughly ignored, but it does pose the question: why did Polaris succeed when so many other projects, both service and civilian and all invariably smaller, fail? It does seem remarkable that a small group of naval officers and civil servants could deliver what was a very involved, costly and complex project. Admiral Mackenzie and his small team not only procured a completely new weapon system, they directed the design and building of a total new class of submarine to carry the missiles, oversaw the building of a new base to accommodate these submarines and their crews, and supervised the construction of an establishment to store and maintain the submarine's nuclear weapons. Added to this were problems concerning finding the personnel to man the submarines and ensuring they had the necessary training. Not only was this completed but completed on time and to budget. Also, the initial concepts and procedures implemented by CPE proved so reliable and sound that they provided the foundations that made it possible for the system to operate successfully for well over its design life.

In view of this I have often wondered why management consultants seem reluctant to use the British Polaris project as an example of a well-managed project. It would seem an ideal training aid for modern business; it covered the whole array of management activities: planning, organisation, logistics, guidance, governance, communications, personnel management, risk management, continuity management, leadership and direction. I would have thought in a world of blue sky thinking, baselining, thinking outside the box, word clouds or even idea showers, a little common and plain 'Navy Speak' might, if nothing else, provide a ray of linguistic illumination.

Despite often being portrayed as an inflexible and dated organisation, the Polaris project depicts the Royal Navy in rather a different light. It reveals an organisation that is responsive, forward-looking and very effective, demonstrating, perhaps, that the traditional naval management system is not as old-fashioned and inappropriate as we are led to believe. Indeed, many modern management ideas bear some striking similarities to long-established Navy practices. For several centuries, the Navy has lived in a constant state of downsizing, apart from the odd exception of a war-fuelled manpower bump. For hundreds of years it has been subjected to regular bouts of restructuring and there is an arguable case to be made that the Navy pioneered many of the current management techniques. In fact, there are many facets of the traditional Navy 'way' that are not too different from what management consultants would have us believe are the 'New Age' panacea for all business problems.

Modern companies place a great deal of importance on mission statements, corporate image and company culture. The Navy has several hundred years of culture and tradition immortalised in books, pictures, songs, films, etc. Nelson's quote: 'No captain can do very wrong if he places his ship alongside that of the enemy' can be considered a classic mission statement. Admiral Mackenzie's own mission statement for the Polaris project can be considered concise, precise and very relevant: 'To deploy on station the first RN Ballistic Submarine with its missiles, and with fully report, in July 1968 and thereafter the remainder at six monthly intervals. These dates cannot be allowed to slip.' A very significant statement of intent.

As companies moved to a 'flatter' management structure, one criticism often levelled at the Royal Navy was the number of rates or grades within the naval chain of command. It could be argued that the number of rates allowed personnel to train for the next rate before they were actually advanced. Admittedly, it is a system born out of necessity during conflict, but not an unsound policy that had a lot in its favour.

To compensate for the flatter management structure often employed in companies, a system called horizontal fast-tracking has been introduced; it is said to be a form of 'sideways elevation' that is meant to offset the limited promotional opportunities in the newer flatter organisations, essentially doing different jobs at the same grade. It is said to lead to a better-trained person with a deeper insight into all aspects of the organisation's structure. This sounds remarkably similar to the naval appointing and drafting systems. This flatter management pyramid is said to improve communications within the company. Most, if not all, sea-going captains operate an open-door policy, where crew members are encouraged to voice any concerns directly to him. It would be difficult to imagine a flatter structure.

Other popular concepts such as decentralisation, leadership training and empowerment are without doubt longstanding and accepted parts of naval life. The 'No Blame Culture' has been the practice, certainly in the Submarine Service, for the last 100 years. With its various watch-keeping systems – watchbills, daily routines, etc. – the Navy was surely a pioneer in the time management field. A further management aim is to standardise procedures, routines, uniform/clothing and ethos throughout the company – surely this is what DCIs, BRs, standing orders, daily orders, and Queen's regulations do? They are the very foundation of naval life; the Royal Navy learned a long time ago that tradition is absorbed, not taught.

Despite its autocratic nature, the Navy was always personnel orientated, even dating back to Victorian times. Nowadays it is a truly holistic organisation, combining administration, welfare, medical and even spiritual aspects of its employees' lives. It is common practice now for many large firms to combine the pay and personnel office functions, similar to the Unit Personnel Office (UPO) some might say. Maybe the Navy should wait a while and let the rest catch up. I believe that, in the not too distant future, a management consultant will become a very rich man selling the Naval Divisional System to an awestruck business world

This background provided Admiral Mackenzie with a sound and extensive grounding in the various fields that made up his job. The same can be said of Napier, Watt, Kingdom Brunel, Stephenson, etc. Mackenzie was a true leader, and while a leader will always be able to manage, certificates and qualifications in the latter don't necessarily confer any degree of competence in the former. Leaders will always manage but I'm not sure the reverse is true. To him; logistics, strategy, organisation, administration, authority and responsibility and unity of command were part of what he did every day, it was part of his normal working life. Mackenzie was held in very high regard, even affection, by his staff. It's been said that there is nobody, civil or military, high or low grade, who was involved in the project, who didn't look back on their days serving under him as the most inspiring in their service career. He also had the ability to win the trust of the Americans and the many industrialists who were involved in the programme. One of his staff said: 'I never came out of CPE's office without feeling better, even if he'd slapped my scheme down.' Unquestionably, it was Mackenzie's leadership abilities that were directly responsible for the success of the Polaris programme.

Mackenzie and his team were not driven by thoughts of ever swelling bonuses, golden hellos or obscene golden goodbyes. He and his team were not, nor would have wanted to have been, the subject of a reality TV show or some fly on the wall documentary. There were no mercenary reasons for their actions other than the satisfaction of doing their duty. They did not see success in terms of personal material gain, they saw success in terms of achievement; a job well done, a duty done and done well. It is a perspective that is at odds or even alien to the ego-driven greed that is the norm for certain sectors of the business world.

This is in part driven by the need to 'specialise' in one particular field. While this is arguably necessary with the ever-increasing complexity of the modern business world, it has one major drawback, it allows the people involved to avoid taking charge; they are not responsible, it can always be argued that it's someone else's job. They can avoid taking overall responsibility and making the necessary decisions. How often do you hear when something goes wrong that they are reviewing procedures? Admiral Rickover was of the opinion that responsibility was a unique concept that could only be vested in a single individual. While it could be shared with a number of others, your individual portion remained the same. Unless, he felt, you could point your finger at the man who was responsible when something went wrong, you never had anybody who was really responsible. Unfortunately, this lack of willingness to accept responsibility has led to over-inflated egos, with the people concerned having an unbelievable overconfidence in their abilities that often appears as indefensible conceit.

And perhaps therein lies the reason why the Polaris project is not used as an example and benchmark standard of a well-run successful project; it questions, if not totally discredits, the old management adage that, to get the best results, you have to pay top dollar. The Polaris team were paid the going rate for their grade or rank, no bonuses or target pay. Their only reward was knowing that it was a job well done. Words, old-fashioned words, such as dependability, integrity, honour, duty, pride and modesty, best describe the underpinning values of the Polaris team's approach to their work. They took full responsibility for their actions, which appears an unfamiliar concept in some areas of modern management. It would be fair to say that this ethos and these qualities, which underpinned the Polaris procurement team's attitude, was more than evident throughout the programme for its whole life. Not only the crews but their families and the people who supported the squadron and its submarines.

It was this point that Prime Minister John Major emphasised in his speech at the End of Polaris Ceremony at Faslane on 28 August 1996:

Secretary of State for Defence, First Sea Lord, Ladies and Gentlemen.

We are here today to pay tribute to the work of the Polaris Force.

The debt we owe is very large. For the last 28 years this Force has mounted continuous patrols that have been vital to ensure this country's peace and security. Because of these patrols, any possible aggressor has known that to attack the UK would provoke a terrible response.

In particular, we are here today to pay tribute to the last of the four Polaris submarines, HMS *Repulse*, which returned from her sixtieth and final deployment in May.

But not only *Repulse*, of course. I pay tribute, too, to the other three boats and their crews in her Class: the *Resolution* herself, *Renown* and *Revenge*. Each has made its own unique and invaluable contribution to the remarkable record of maintaining a Polaris submarine at sea, on deterrent patrol, undetected by friend or foe, every day, of every year, from 1969 until May this year.

To those of you who have served aboard any of these submarines, past and present, I offer you the thanks not just of those others of us here but of people throughout the country.

The years of the Polaris Force have seen some dramatic changes. In 1968, when *Resolution* began her first patrol, East/West tension was running high. The Soviet Union had invaded Czechoslovakia and the Vietnam War raged. And yet, in 1994, I signed an accord with President Yeltsin agreeing no longer to target our nuclear forces at each other's territory. Today, the West enjoys a co-operative relationship with Russia unthinkable even ten years ago.

But throughout the turbulent years the Polaris force has always been there, always ready, always prepared, always the ultimate guarantee of this country's security.

As I said, the debt is very great.

No tribute to those of you in the SSBN force, however, would be complete without a special mention of the contribution of your families at home. They, as well as you, have borne the continual strain of enforced separation. They have had to maintain the family while you were gone, relying for communication only on the forty words of the weekly 'familygram'. None of the achievements of the Polaris fleet would have been possible without their forbearance and their understanding. To them, too, I offer a very special thank you and I am glad that so many are here today.

I would like to thank, too, all those who maintain the submarine and its deterrent away from the boat itself, whether at the base here, in Coulport supporting the weapons system, on the tugs moving these massive submarines in and out of port, at the headquarters at Northwood, or in the design and support organisations further afield. Each of you has played your part.

Throughout the Polaris programme we have enjoyed very close co-operation with the United States. This will continue with Trident. Our two Navies have a very special trust and understanding. I am delighted that so many representatives of the United States Strategic Systems Programme are with us today, together with the officers and crew of the USS *West Virginia*.

There is naturally a tinge of sadness today. But it is the ending of a chapter only. As Trident takes over from Polaris and Chevaline, so the Vanguard Class takes on the torch from *Resolution* and her sisters.

Let me say a word about our deterrent.

I have no doubt that we are right to maintain a minimum credible strategic nuclear deterrent for the United Kingdom. We will continue to do so for as long as our security needs require. It would be folly for us not to do so. *Vanguard* and *Victorious* are already fully operational and meeting all our expectations. I look forward to seeing them joined, in 1998, by *Vigilant* and, around the turn of the century, by *Vengeance*. Together, these four submarines will carry the UK's strategic and sub-strategic deterrent well into the twenty-first century.

In a few moments I shall unveil this plaque marking the proud achievements of the Polaris Force. And, as I unveil it here, so, at the entrance to this facility a little way away, a small stone monument is also being unveiled. This monument is to serve as a quiet and dignified reminder of the unique contribution made to peace and security by these submarines and the men who served in them.

We should be unashamedly proud of the Polaris project. During its thirty-seven-year life the Polaris fleet carried out 229 deterrent patrols, maintaining the country's Continuous At Sea Deterrent. Polaris delivered all through its life and was well led at all levels, be that commanding officers, officers, senior rates and junior rates. It was undeniably well supported by base maintenance staff. The crew's families played an undeniably major role and bore an unimaginable burden during on-crew periods.

The Polaris project also has another claim to fame that shouldn't be forgotten: it was possibly the last time that the Navy was fun.

ACKNOWLEDGEMENTS

I am very grateful to the following people and organisations for their assistance and support while I was compiling this book: Richard Evans for the loan of his memorabilia and permission to use it; Tony Smyth for his photos, stories and more importantly his friendship over the years, and not forgetting his daily weather updates from Malta; Arry Hartnett, for permission to use his vacuum cleaner story; also, the members of the West of Scotland Submariners Association for sharing their stories with me and putting up with my endless questions, particularly Lt Cdr Ron Laley former WEO HMS *Repulse* and Chris Leggett Cdr RN MBE for his help with the photographs

Special thanks to Commander Bob Seaward OBE Royal Navy, who not only suppled photos, dits and friendly advice but also very kindly agreed to write the foreword.

I'd like to thank Gerry McFeely, for his support, for checking the original manuscript and for sharing his recollections of the Signing of the Polar Agreement Ceremony; Keith S. Hall for his help with the editing the manuscript and for being my son; and José Piët for proofreading the final draft.

Many thanks to Bill Smith for permission to use his pictures, particularly the very emotive cover picture; Sam Morrow for his help with the ships crests; Vanessa Burgess, from the Office of the Rt Hon Sir John Major KG CH, for permission to reproduce in full the speech Sir John made at the End of Polaris Ceremony at Faslane; The four Resolution-class submarine websites for permission to rummage through their sites and purloin the contents; George Griffiths and his website 'Submariners Lounge' for access to the pictures and a vast number of dits; Nick Barwis for supplying the SM 10 and SM 1 crests, from his website Jacktaxi.

All MOD pictures and quotes from official documents are reproduced under the Governments Open Licence scheme. Contains public sector information licensed under the Open Government Licence v3.0.

As always, I must also thank The History Press for once again allowing me to tell my story, and in particular Amy Rigg and Lauren Newby for their help and advice, and the massive undertaking of making sense of my jumbled and disorganised manuscript.

There are undoubtedly many people who have contributed to this book whom I have failed to acknowledge, primarily the submarine crews themselves. I apologise and thank you all; over the years you have amused, bemused and confused me in equal measure. But most importantly, I have had the honour to meet and work with a lot of wonderful people and I made a lot of very good friends. We were members of a very exclusive club. Following HMS *Resolution*'s epic patrol, it would be fair to say that more people had been to space than have spent that long under the sea. I'm not sure you could experience the ethos of comradery, professionalism and leadership anywhere else.

And finally, my thanks to the lady I met when I returned from my first Polaris patrol and who, more importantly, waited for me to return after every other one, Hilary.

I hope this reflects, in some small way, the effort, commitment and competence of all the personnel involved in the Polaris program.

BIBLIOGRAPHY

Britain and the H Bomb, Lorna Arnold.

Keeping the Peace: The Aldermaston Story, David J. Hawkins.

Nuclear Diplomacy and the Special Relationship, Ian Clark.

The Clyde Submarine Base, Keith Hall.

Launch Pad UK, Jim Wilson OBE.

The Royal Navy and Nuclear Weapons, Richard Moore.

'The Royal Navy's Polaris lobby, 1955–62', Ken Young, *Journal of Strategic Studies* (2002), 25: 3, pp. 56–86.

Independence and Interdependence, Edited by John Poole.

Nuclear Weapons and British Strategic Planning 1955–1958, Martin S. Navias.

The Nassau Connection, Peter Nailor.

The Labour Party Defence Policy since 1945, Dan Keohane.

ALSO BY THE AUTHOR

Around the Gareloch and Rosneath Peninsular
ISBN: 978-0-7524-2106-3

HM Naval Base Clyde
ISBN: 978-0-7524-6480-0

HMS Defiance
ISBN: 978-0-7523-3758-3

HMS Dolphin: Gosport's Submarine Base
ISBN: 978-0-7524-2113-1

Gareloch and Rosneath (Pocket Images)
ISBN: 978-1-8458-8402-4

Rosneath and Gareloch: Then and Now
ISBN: 978-0-7524-2389-0658

Submariners News: The Peculiar Press of the Underwater Mariner
ISBN: 978-0-7524-5793-2

Submariners: Real Life Stories from the Deep
ISBN: 978-0-7524-2809-3

The Clyde Submarine Base: Images of Scotland
ISBN: 978-0-7524-1657-1

FRIENDS OF THE ROYAL NAVY SUBMARINE MUSEUM

Royalties from this publication will be paid to the Friends of the Royal Navy Submarine Museum.

With the 1998 demise of HMS *Dolphin*, the original alma mater, the Royal Navy Submarine Museum established at Haslar Jetty in the 1980s has become the natural link with submarine history, stretching back to the beginning of the last century.

Featuring the first Royal Navy submarine *Holland 1* and HMS *Alliance* of Second World War vintage, the museum provides a comprehensive record of the life and times of the Submarine Branch of the Royal Navy.

Well-established as a major visitor attraction, the museum also boasts a significant research facility, with some 50,000 documents, 120,000 photographs, 300 works of art and 800 medals and the collection continues to grow.

The cost of preserving this important part of our heritage for the future always exceeds the available budget and this is where the Friends make such a vital contribution.

Founded with charitable status in 1995 (Registered Charity No. 1046251), the Society of Friends has attracted more than 700 members and the support of the Hampshire County Council. With a sound financial base, the Society has an ongoing programme to finance the conservation of photographs and other archive material, enhancing display galleries, staff training and the purchase of submarine-related artefacts.

The Friends are an active, involved society, working to preserve the heritage of the Submarine Service through its museum. Recent initiatives supported by the Friends have been the Submarine Memorial Garden, the VC Exhibition and the Submarine Book of Remembrance.